Drew Provan

iPad

covers iOS 7
for iPad 2 – 5 (iPad Air) and iPad Mini

In easy steps is an imprint of In Easy Steps Limited
16 Hamilton Terrace · Holly Walk · Leamington Spa
Warwickshire · United Kingdom · CV32 4LY
www.ineasysteps.com

Fifth Edition

Notice of Liability
Every effort has been made to ensure that this book contains accurate
and current information. However, In Easy Steps Limited and the
author shall not be liable for any loss or damage suffered by readers
as a result of any information contained herein.

Trademarks
All trademarks are acknowledged as belonging to their respective
companies.

In Easy Steps Limited supports The Forest Stewardship Council (FSC),
the leading international forest certification organisation. All our titles
that are printed on Greenpeace approved FSC certified paper carry the
FSC logo.

MIX
Paper from
responsible sources
FSC® C020837

Printed and bound in the United Kingdom

ISBN 978-1-84078-609-5

Contents

7 Videos 113

8 Podcasts 123

9 Calendar 129

1 Welcome to Your New iPad!

The iPad is a multimedia tablet like no other. Its rich graphics and seamless integration with iTunes make it perfect for work and play. Most tasks requiring a laptop can be carried out on the iPad, (with its iOS 7 operating system) which is light, power-efficient, instantly-on and incredibly intuitive to use. It also has an huge number of third-party apps to expand its already impressive capabilities and performance.

Welcome to the iPad!

Congratulations on buying an iPad, a sophisticated multimedia tablet computer capable of playing music, dealing with emails, browsing the Web, organizing your calendar and thousands of other applications! Or maybe you haven't bought an iPad yet but are considering doing so. Let's look at what you can use the iPad for:

- Listening to music

- Recording and watching videos

- Taking photos

- Reading ebooks

- Browsing the Web

- Emails, contacts and calendars

- Social networking

- FaceTime video chats, playing games, and much more

Will it replace my laptop?

Probably not, although for many functions it can be used instead of a laptop. It depends on what you use your laptop for. If you mainly do web browsing, check emails and use social networking apps then the iPad can easily replace your laptop. If, on the other hand, you use your laptop to generate PowerPoint slides or create complex documents then the iPad may not be ideal, since some functions are missing from the iPad.

What's missing from the iPad?

There are features found on laptops and desktops that are missing from the iPad. At present there is no:

- SD card slot

- USB slots (though the Apple Camera Kit does have a 30-pin plug which has a USB socket at one end, but this is to connect your camera rather than attach other devices)

- The ability to access files and drag them around or drop into folders is not available on the iPad. You can get files on there but it's clunky and not very intuitive

Depending on your needs, the iPad may not be a laptop replacement. Assess your needs carefully before buying one!

Apple's website has Q and As and lots of helpful tips on using the iPad.

The New icon pictured above indicates a new or enhanced feature introduced on the iPad with the latest version iOS 7.

iPad Specifications

Since its introduction there are now several different generations of iPad, including the iPad Mini, which is smaller than the original iPad. When considering which iPad is best for you some of the specifications to consider are:

- **Processor:** This determines the speed at which the iPad operates and how quickly tasks are performed.

- **Storage:** This determines how much content you can store on your iPad. Across the iPad family, the range of storage is 16GB, 32GB, 64GB or 128GB.

- **Connectivity:** The options for this are Wi-Fi and 3G/4G connectivity for the Internet and Bluetooth for connecting to other devices over short distances. All models of iPad have Wi-Fi connectivity as standard.

- **Screen:** Look for an iPad with a Retina Display screen for the highest resolution and best clarity. This is an LED-backlit screen and is available on the latest iPads.

- **Operating System**. The full size version of the iPad and the iPad Mini both run on the iOS 7 operating system.

- **Battery power:** This is the length of time the iPad can be used for general use such as surfing the Web on Wi-Fi, watching video, or listening to music. All models offer approximately 10 hours of use in this way.

- **Input/Output:** Both the iPad and the iPad Mini have similar output/input options. These are a lightning connector port (for charging), 3.5 mm stereo headphone minijack, built-in speaker, microphone and micro-SIM card tray (Wi-Fi and 4G model only).

- **Sensors:** These are used to access the amount of ambient light and also the orientation in which the iPad is being held. The sensors are accelerometer, ambient light sensor and gyroscope.

- **TV and video:** This determines how your iPad can be connected to a High Definition TV. This is done with AirPlay Mirroring.

Hot tip

iOS 7 can be used on all iPads from the iPad 2 upwards and all versions of the iPad Mini.

Beware

If you have a fourth generation iPad (or later) then it'll come with the new lightning connector. You'll need to buy adapters to connect it to your "old" 30-pin accessories, such as TV, iPod dock, etc.

Lightning Connector Adapter

Lightning Connector

30-pin dock Connector

What's New in iOS 7?

iOS 7 is the operating system for the iPad and it brings in many new features. The whole interface has been redesigned to give it a more up-to-date and vibrant appearance and, although there are no new preinstalled apps, there have been a number of improvements in the existing ones to ensure that iOS 7 is the most advanced mobile operating system out there.

A quick round-up of the features of iOS 7 is shown below:

New design

iOS 7 is one of the most dramatic cosmetic changes to the operating system in its history. It was overseen by the designer Jonathan Ive, who was responsible for some of the most iconic Apple devices including the iMac, iPod and iPhone. The design is intended to be a cleaner, simpler one for the icons and apps and moves away from previous styles, which relied on the interpretation of everyday materials such as paper, leather, wood and felt.

The interpretation of everyday items in the design of computer interfaces is known as skeuomorphic.

Control Center

This is a way of quickly accessing some of the commonly used functions on the iPad. It can be activated by swiping up from the bottom of any screen.

Multitasking

Some previous versions of iOS had a multitasking bar, but this has been redesigned in iOS 7 so that it provides a full screen option for viewing and using your open apps and also closing the ones that you do not want to currently use.

Camera and Photos

This includes options for taking photos in different ratios, a new way of organizing and viewing your photos in the Photos app and special effects added to the editing functions.

Siri improvements

The voice assistant function that was introduced in iOS 6 has been improved further with a new interface and a wider range of content over which it can search.

Safari improvements

The iOS 7 web browser now has a unified Search/Address bar, an improved tabs view and shared links so that you can view your social networking updates through Safari.

App Store improvements

The iPad App Store has been redesigned and includes a new feature that can show apps that are particularly relevant to your current location.

Don't forget

iOS 7 also has improvements to the Find My iPhone (or iPad) service and a range of options for business users, including improved security for personal data.

Finding Your Way Around

The physical buttons and controls on the iPad are very simple. Additional functions such as screen brightness are software-controlled.

Status bar   FaceTime camera   Sleep/Wake/On/Off

Micro-SIM tray (some models)

App icons

Home button

iSight Camera   Microphone   Headset Jack

Side switch

Side switch

Volume Up/ Down

Volume

Speaker   Lightning connector

The **network data icons** at the top of the screen are pretty much like those found on the iPhone.

iPad ❖	14:13	❋ 36% ▭▯
Settings	**Bluetooth**	
✈ Airplane Mode ⬤	Bluetooth	⬤
🛜 Wi-Fi NETGEAR	DEVICES	
✳ Bluetooth On	Searching...	

The fastest data connection is Wi-Fi. If no Wi-Fi is available you will need to use 3G/4G which is fairly fast. Unfortunately, as you move around, the 3G/4G signal will come and go so you may see the 3G/4G disappear and be replaced by the EDGE symbol (E). EDGE is slower than 3G/4G.

If you're *really* unlucky the EDGE signal may vanish and you may see the GPRS symbol. GPRS is *very* slow!

o	GPRS (slowest)	➚	Location services
E	EDGE	🔒	Lock
3G	3G	LTE	LTE
4G	4G	☁	Personal Hotspot
🛜	Wi-Fi	▶	Play
✳	Bluetooth	⊡	Screen lock
✈	Airplane mode	↻	Syncing
❊	iPad is busy		

The GPRS, EDGE and 3G/4G icons are seen on the Wi-Fi and cellular models only.

Home Button and Screen

There are very few actual physical buttons on the iPad but the Home button is an important one. The Home button functions changed since the arrival of iOS 4.2, allowing you to see active apps in the Multitasking bar.

You can quit active multitasking apps (this was not possible with earlier versions of iPad).

Hot tip

You can see your active apps by bringing up the Multitasking window. If an app is misbehaving, quit it using the Multitasking window.

16

Hot tip

To see the Multitasking window without having to press the Home Button twice, drag four fingers up the screen. You can also drag four fingers right or left across the screen to switch between open apps.

- If you are on the Home screen (the first screen) press and hold the Home button to activate the Siri voice search assistant function

- If you are on any other screen press the Home button to go back to the Home screen: this saves you having to flick the screens to the left

- When using the Music application with Home button it minimizes the Music window allowing you to use other applications while listening to music

- Pressing the Home button quickly twice brings up the Multitasking window (shows your active apps)

...cont'd

The **Home screen** is the first screen you see when you start up the iPad. It contains the apps installed by Apple (and these cannot be deleted). In all, there are 20 of these – 4 will be on the Dock.

The Dock comes with four apps attached. You can move these off, add other apps (the Dock can hold a maximum of six apps or folders), or you can put your favorite apps there and remove those placed on the Dock by Apple.

You can move these apps to other screens if you want to but it's a good idea to keep the most important or most frequently-used apps on this screen.

You might expect iBooks (to buy ebooks) to be a preinstalled app but in fact you have to go to the App Store and download this free app if you want to use the iPad as an ebook reader.

Network connections   Time   Battery

Wallpaper

Preinstalled apps   iPad screens   Apps on the Dock (up to 6)

Hot tip

By default there are four apps on the Dock at the bottom of the screen. You can add two more if needed.

You can even drag folders to the Dock.

Multitasking Window

The iPad can run several programs at once and these can be managed by the Multitasking window. This has been redesigned for iOS 7 and it performs a number of tasks:

- It shows open apps

- It enables you to move between open apps and open different ones

- It enables apps to be closed (see next page)

Accessing Multitasking

The Multitasking option can be accessed from any screen on your iPad, as follows:

1 Double-click on the **Home** button

2 The currently-open apps are displayed, with their icons underneath them (except the Home screen). The most recently-used apps are shown first

3 Swipe left and right to view the open apps. Tap on one to access it in full screen size

Closing Items

The iPad deals with open apps very efficiently. They do not interact with other apps, which increases security and also means that they can be open in the background, without using up a significant amount of processing power, in a state of semi-hibernation until they are needed. Because of this it is not essential to close apps when you move to something else. However, you may want to close apps if you feel you have too many open or if one stops working. To do this:

1 Access the Multitasking window. The currently-open apps are displayed

2 Press and hold on an app and swipe it to the top of the screen to close it. This does not remove it from the iPad and it can be opened again in the usual way

3 The app is removed from its position in the Multitasking window

In the Control Center

The Control Center is a panel containing some of the most commonly used options within the **Settings** app. It can be accessed with one swipe and is an excellent function for when you do not want to have to go into Settings.

Accessing the Control Center

The Control Center can be accessed from any screen within iOS 7 and it can also be accessed from the Lock Screen:

 Tap on the **Settings** app

The Control Center cannot be disabled from being accessed from the Home screen.

 Tap once on the **Control Center** tab and drag the **Access on Lock Screen** and **Access Within Apps** buttons On or Off to specify if the Control Center can be accessed from there (if both are Off, it can still be accessed from any Home screen)

 Swipe up from the bottom of any screen to access the Control Center panel

 Tap on this button to hide the Control Center panel, or tap anywhere on the screen

...cont'd

Control Center controls

The items that can be used in the Control Center are:

1 Use these controls for any music or video that is playing. Use the buttons to Pause/Play a track, go to the beginning or end and adjust the volume

2 Tap once on this button to turn **Airplane mode** On or Off

3 Tap once on this button to turn **Wi-Fi** On or Off

4 Tap once on this button to turn **Bluetooth** On or Off

5 Tap once on this button to turn **Do Not Disturb** mode On or Off

6 Tap once on this button to access a clock, including a stopwatch

7 Tap once on this button to open the **Camera** app

8 Use this slider to adjust the screen brightness

9 Tap once on this button to **Lock** or **Unlock** screen rotation. If it is locked, the screen will not change when you change the orientation of your iPad

Hot tip

The screen rotation can also be locked from within the **General** section of the **Settings** app. Under **Use Side Switch to**, tap once on the **Lock Rotation** link. Then the side switch can be used to lock, and unlock, the screen rotation.

Finding Things on the iPad

Sometimes you haven't got time to look through your entire calendar for an appointment, or to scroll through iTunes for one track. You can use Spotlight (Apple's indexing and search facility) to find specific apps, contacts, emails, appointments and Music content.

Start search

Hot tip

Search using Spotlight to avoid spending ages looking for emails, music tracks and other data.

1 From any free area on a Home screen, press and hold and swipe downwards

2 You will be taken to the Spotlight search screen

3 Enter your search word or string into the search box

4 Your results will show up below. The results are grouped according to their type, i.e. Calendar appointment, email, etc.

Finding Things with Siri

Siri is the iPad voice assistant that provides answers to a variety of questions by looking at your iPad and also web services. You can ask Siri questions relating to the apps on your iPad and also general questions, such as weather conditions around the world, or sports results. To set up:

 Open **Settings > General**, tap on the **Siri** link

2 Drag the **Siri** button to **On** to activate the Siri functionality

Questioning Siri

Once you have set up Siri, you can start putting it to work with your queries. To do this:

1 Hold down the **Home** button until the Siri window appears

What can I help you with?

2 If you do not ask anything initially, Siri will prompt you with some suggestions (or tap on the ? button in the bottom left-hand corner for more suggestions)

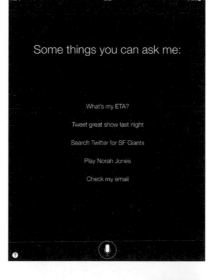
Some things you can ask me:

What's my ETA?

Tweet great show last night

Search Twitter for SF Giants

Play Norah Jones

Check my email

3 Tap once on the microphone button to ask a question of Siri

Default Applications

These are the preinstalled apps:

Hot tip

iBooks is Apple's ebook reader and is not preinstalled; you need to go to the App Store and download it (free).

Calendar: keeps your appointments in sync with your PC or Mac using wired or wireless sync

Contacts: list of all contacts including phone numbers, email, postal addresses and notes

Notes: for jotting things down. Sync with your computer or you can email them to yourself

Maps: GPS-enabled maps help you get from A to B, current position, and other information

Videos: play movies and other video content, purchased or from your own collection

iTunes Store: browse and buy music, movies, TV shows and more

App Store: your central store for paid and free apps

Reminders: to-do lists, sync with Apple Mail and Outlook Tasks

Messages: send SMS-type messages free with Wi-Fi

Settings: this is where you make changes to personalize your iPad

Safari: Apple's home-grown web browser

Mail: handles IMAP and POP3 email, and syncs to your main accounts on your computer

Photos: show your photos with slideshows, print off photos or share via Facebook, Twitter, etc.

Music: controls music, podcasts, etc.

Game Center: social gaming, lets you play games and interact with friends

Camera: shoot stills or movies using front or back cameras similar to iPhone functionality

FaceTime: video chat to others using iPad, iPhone 4 and 5 or Mac

Photo Booth: take still images and select from a series of special effects

Newsstand: stores your newspaper and magazine subscriptions

Clock: provides time in any part of the world. Useful as an alarm clock and a stopwatch

The Display and Keyboard

What's all the excitement about the screen? What makes it so special?

The technology behind the multi-touch screen is ingenious. Using one, two, three or four fingers you can do lots of different things on the iPad depending on the app you're using and what you want to do. The main actions are tap, flick, pinch/spread and drag.

The screen is designed to be used with fingers – the skin on glass contact is required (if you tap using your nail you will find it won't work). There are styluses you can buy for the iPad but for full functionality, fingers on screen give the best results.

Tap	Apps open when you tap their icons. Within apps you can select photos, music, web links and many other functions. The tap is similar to a single click with a mouse on the computer
Flick	You can flick through lists like Contacts, Songs, or anywhere there's a long list. Place your finger on the screen and quickly flick up and down and the list scrolls rapidly up and down
Pinch/spread	The iPad screen responds to two fingers placed on its surface. To reduce the size of a photo or web page in Safari place two fingers on the screen and bring them together. To enlarge the image or web page spread your fingers apart and the image grows in size
Drag	You can drag web pages and maps around if you are unable to see the edges. Simply place your finger on the screen and keep it there but move the image or web page around until you can see the hidden areas

Beware

The screen responds best to skin contact. Avoid using pens or other items to tap the screen.

Hot tip

Use four fingers to bring up the Multitasking window (drag four fingers up the screen), or flick right or left using four fingers to switch between running apps.

…cont'd

The iPad is different to a laptop since there is no physical keyboard. Instead you type by tapping the **virtual keyboard** on the iPad screen itself. You can use the keyboard in portrait or landscape modes. The landscape version provides much wider keys.

The keyboard seems to change in different apps

The keyboard is smart – and should match the app you're in. For example, if you are word processing or entering regular text you will see a standard keyboard. But if you are using a browser or are prompted to enter an email address you will see a modified keyboard with *.com* and @ symbols prominently displayed.

Hot tip

If you have Wi-Fi, try using your voice to dictate emails and other text using the Dictate option (its icon is on the left of the spacebar).

26

Top left: portrait keyboard in Mail.

Top right: portrait keyboard in Pages.

Bottom left: portrait keyboard in Safari – note the **Return** key has now changed to **Go**. Tap this to search the web or go to a specific URL.

If you find you are making lots of typing errors, try switching the iPad to landscape mode (keys are larger).

Mail with iPad in the landscape position. Notice how wide the keys have become, making it easier to type without hitting two keys at once! Also notice the Dictation icon to the left of the spacebar (you get this when on Wi-Fi).

27

Don't forget

The keyboard in the Apple productivity apps, Pages, Keynote and Numbers, still uses the old-style keyboard, which has the same functionality but has gray keys instead of white ones.

Pages with landscape keyboard. Again, the keyboard is large but the downside is that you lose real estate for work – the effective area for viewing content is quite small. Dictation is active – you can tell because the icon has enlarged and shows the volume level as you dictate your text.

Caps Lock and Auto-Correct

It's annoying when you want to type something entirely in upper case letters since you have to press Shift for every letter – or do you? Actually, there's a setting which will activate Caps Lock but you need to activate this in settings:

- Go to **Settings**

- Select **General**

- Select **Keyboard**

- Make sure the **Enable Caps Lock** slider is set to **On**

- While you are there, make sure the other settings are on, for example "." **Shortcut** – this helps you add a period by tapping the spacebar twice (much like the BlackBerry)

Other settings for the keyboard

- **Auto-Correction** suggests the correct word. If it annoys you, switch it off

- **Auto-Capitalization** is great for putting capitals in names

- The "." **Shortcut** types a period every time you hit the spacebar twice. This saves time when typing long emails but if you prefer not to use this, switch it off. Here's another neat trick – you can also insert a period by tapping the spacebar with two fingers simultaneously

...cont'd

As you type words, the iPad **Auto-Correct** will suggest words intelligently which will speed up your typing.

To accept iPad suggestion

When the suggested word pops up, simply tap the space bar and it will be inserted. The suggested word may not be what you want, in which case you can reject it by tapping the 'x'.

To reject suggestion

Above left: iPad will suggest a word but if you don't want to use the suggestion tap the 'x'. The word you type will be added to your user dictionary. Above right: You can look up the dictionary: tap word twice, tap the right arrow and choose Define.

All contact names are automatically added to your user dictionary.

Can I Use a Real Keyboard?

There are times when you need real physical keys, for example if you are typing a longer document you might find tapping out your text on the glass screen annoying. Apple has designed a dock with an integrated keyboard, which is great for holding your iPad at the correct angle, and allowing your iPad to be charged while you type using the keyboard.

Original Apple iPad Keyboard and dock

Don't forget

For some older keyboards you will need the Lightning to 30-pin Adapter.

Hot tip

If you need to type long documents consider using a physical keyboard.

ZAGGmate keyboard for iPad 2 (works with later models too)

Can I use a Bluetooth keyboard?

Absolutely! The iPad has Bluetooth built-in so you can hook up an Apple Bluetooth keyboard and type away. Alternatively, there are third-party keyboards such as the ZAGGmate Bluetooth keyboard (**www.zagg.com**) which acts as a case when not in use (protects the front of the iPad but not the back).

Keyboard Tricks

Although it's not immediately obvious, the keyboard can generate accents, acutes, and many other foreign characters and symbols.

Holding the letter "u" or "e" generates lots of variants. Just slide your finger along till you reach the one you want and it will be inserted into the document.

For accents and other additional characters, touch the key then slide your finger to the character you want to use.

Also, when you use Safari you don't have to enter ".co.uk" in URLs – the **?** key will produce other endings if you touch and hold the key.

Select, Copy and Paste Text

Rather than retype text, you can select text (or pictures) and paste these into other documents or the URL field in Safari. Touch and hold text, images or URL (links) to open, save or copy them.

To select text

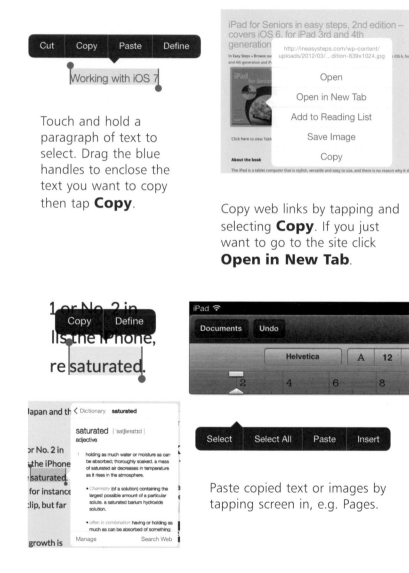

Touch and hold a paragraph of text to select. Drag the blue handles to enclose the text you want to copy then tap **Copy**.

Copy web links by tapping and selecting **Copy**. If you just want to go to the site click **Open in New Tab**.

Paste copied text or images by tapping screen in, e.g. Pages.

Use the built-in dictionary by tapping a word then Define.

Making Corrections

Sometimes words get mistyped. You could retype the whole word but it's easier to correct. Since the iPad isn't a laptop there is no mouse and pointer so you need to get the cursor next to the incorrect character. You can then delete that character and replace it with the correct character.

To position the cursor where you want it

1 Put your finger onto the incorrect word (you may need to tap and hold)

2 Keep your finger on the screen and slide your finger along the word until the cursor is just ahead of the incorrect letter(s)

3 Backspace (delete from right to left) and delete the incorrect character(s)

4 Insert the correct character(s) then locate the end of your text and tap the screen to position the cursor at the end so you can start typing again

5 The iPad can help you if you don't know how to spell the word (tap **Replace...** and it will suggest some words)

Hot tip

You can also correct by double-tapping the incorrectly-spelled word and choosing **Replace** then selecting the correct word.

Making Folders

You will accumulate lots of free and paid apps which will occupy several iPad screens. When you have many apps it can be difficult finding the one you want since you have to flick across several screens to find the right one.

Apple has made it easier to organize your apps by providing the option of creating folders. You might want a folder for games, one for social networking, serious work, and other activities.

Creating a folder

 1 **Hold an app** until all the apps start jiggling on the screen (you will see a small circle on the top left with an **x** – tap the **x** to delete the app)

2 To create a games folder, **touch and hold** a travel app and **drag it** onto another travel app. One will disappear into the other and a folder will be created with the name *Travel*. Rename it if you want to

3 Do this for all the different folders you want to create, e.g. Travel and Games, then tap the Home button. This stops the apps jiggling

You don't need to accept the folder name chosen by the iPad – rename it to whatever you want.

Dragging one app onto another has created a folder called Travel.

Here are the contents of the Games folder. To close the folder, tap outside the folder.

2 Getting Started

As with most technology, although the iPad is plug-and-play, there is some initial setting up to do. It's worth spending some time setting up the iPad so it suits your needs.

Turn On and Register

You can put your iPad fully off or into sleep mode (sleep mode is useful because as soon as you press the Home button the iPad is instantly on).

- If the iPad is fully off, press and hold the **On/Off** button – the iPad will boot up

- When you have finished using it simply press the **On/Off** button briefly and the iPad will enter sleep mode again

- Sleep mode uses very little power so for the sake of speed simply use sleep mode unless you are not going to use the iPad for several days

- To wake from sleep, press the **Home button** or **On/Off** switch

To fully power off

 Press and hold the **On/Off** button until you see the slider bar and **Slide to Power Off** appears

 Slide the red slider to the right

 The iPad will fully shut down

Lock the screen

The iPad works in portrait (upright) and landscape (sideways) modes. The iPad is clever and can tell which way up it is being held and the screen will rotate accordingly. Sometimes you will want it to stay fixed in portrait or landscape modes. This can be done with the Screen Lock function. This can be controlled by the Control Center. To do this, swipe up from the bottom of the screen and tap on this button.

...cont'd

Like the iPhone, the iPad needs to be **registered** with Apple before you can use it.

To register

1 Plug the iPad into your computer (Mac or PC) using the sync cable provided and iTunes should open automatically. If not, double-click app to **launch iTunes** manually

2 The Devices tab on the right side of the iTunes window should show the **iPad**. You will then see the **Welcome to Your New iPad** pane in iTunes

3 Click **Continue** to reach the next screen

4 **Accept the license conditions** and click **Continue**

5 The next pane requests your iTunes account ID and password. If you do not have an iTunes account click the **I do not have an Apple ID** option. Click **Continue**

6 The next page will ask if you want to use iCloud for Push Email/Calendar and Contacts

7 Either choose to use your existing iCloud account, or register for one, or if you don't want iCloud select **Not Now**

8 The next pane lets you **Name** your iPad and decide how you want to sync your data (songs, videos, and other content) to the iPad

9 If you want songs and videos to sync automatically check the boxes marked **Automatically Sync Songs and Videos to My iPad**, **Automatically Add Photos to my iPad**, and **Automatically Sync Applications to my iPad**

Hot tip

You can register your iPad directly from the iPad too. You will need to be online. Go to **Settings > iTunes & App Store. Tap Create Apple ID** and follow the instructions that appear on your iPad. However, it is a good idea to plug the iPad into your Mac or PC regularly so you have a recent backup of all your files, music, and apps.

Syncing Your Data

Your iPad can store several types of information:

- Calendar

- Email

- Contacts

- Music

- Photos

- Videos

- Podcasts

- Apps (applications, i.e. programs)

- Documents

Automated syncs take the guesswork out of syncing.

In some cases this information will mainly reside on your computer. In order to keep all of your information up-to-date you may want to sync it between your computer and your iPad. This can be done in two ways:

- With the online iCloud service

- Using iTunes on a Mac computer or PC

With iCloud, items such as Calendars, Contacts and Reminders get synced automatically once it has been set up. With iTunes you can sync items such as Music, Movies, TV Shows, Podcasts and iBooks. You will need to choose which media files and apps get synced when you plug your iPad into your computer. You can also select to have iTunes sync your content automatically or do it manually for more control.

When you connect your iPad to your computer it will show up under the **Devices** heading in the iTunes sidebar.

- You can opt *not* to open iTunes automatically when you plug the iPad in

- You can also choose to sync some types of content *manually* rather than automatically

Options

- ☐ Open iTunes when this iPad is connected
- ☐ Sync with this iPad over Wi-Fi
- ☐ Sync only checked songs and videos
- ☐ Prefer standard definition videos
- ☐ Convert higher bit rate songs to | 128 kbps ⬍ | **AAC**
- ☑ Manually manage music and videos
- [Reset Warnings]
- [Configure Accessibility...]

Using iCloud

Apple iCloud

This is a service that allows you to use the cloud to sync your data (calendars, contacts, mail, Safari bookmarks, and notes) wirelessly.

Once you are registered and set up, any entries or deletions to calendars and other apps are reflected in all devices using iCloud.

An Apple ID is required for using iCloud, and this can be obtained online at **https://appleid.apple.com/** or you can create an Apple ID when you first access an app on your iPad that requires this for use. It is free to create an Apple ID and requires a username and password. Once you have created an Apple ID you can then use the full range of iCloud services.

Start using iCloud on the iPad and computers

1 Open the iCloud System Preferences (Mac) or Control Panel (PC)

2 Log into your iCloud account with your Apple ID (you only need to do this once – it will remember your details)

3 Check **On** the items that you want synced by iCloud

4 On your iPad, open the **Settings > iCloud** and select the items you want to be used by iCloud. All of the selected items will be reflected on the equivalent apps on your computer

The iPad apps that require an Apple ID to access their full functionality include: iTunes Store, iMessages, iBooks, FaceTime and the App Store.

...cont'd

Using iCloud online

Once you have created an Apple ID you will automatically have an iCloud account. This can be used to sync your data from your iPad and you can also access your content online from the iCloud website at **www.icloud.com**

 Enter your Apple ID details

 Click the iCloud button from any section to go to other areas

 The full range of iCloud apps is displayed, including those for Pages, Numbers and Keynote

Click on an app to view its details. If iCloud is set up on your iPad, any changes made here will be displayed in the online app too

Find my iPad

This is a great feature which allows you to see where your devices are. Once activated (**Settings > iCloud > Find my iPad**), log into iCloud using a browser and click Find My iPhone. This will find your iPad and any other devices you have registered.

Hot tip

iCloud provides 5GB free storage but you can pay for more. (*Correct at the time of printing.*)For example, I upgraded my iCloud storage to 25GB.

Syncing with iTunes

As well as using iCloud to sync your content you can also use iTunes on a Mac or PC to sync certain types of content, including:

- Music
- Videos
- Apps
- TV shows
- Podcast
- Books

If you have synced music, movies, TV shows and books from other iTunes libraries you will see a warning message when you try and sync these items from a new library, warning that previously synced items will be removed. Click on the **Remove and Sync** button to continue.

 Click on your iPad under the Devices heading in the iTunes sidebar. Click on the top toolbar to access the different content to sync

Syncing Apps

This is useful so that you have a backup of the apps in case you need to restore the iPad.

 Click the **Apps** pane in iTunes when the iPad is connected to your computer

 Click the **Install** button if you want to add an app to your iPad. Apps can also be added by dragging them to the screen on the right-hand side

3 On the right-hand side you will see a mini-representation of all the screens on your iPad with the apps in their positions on the screens

4 Use the mini-screen windows to move your apps to wherever you want to place them (you can do this on the iPad, too, but it is much easier on the computer)

5 Click the **Sync** button at the bottom right of the iTunes window to sync the apps between iPad and computer

To move lots of apps it's much easier to use the mini-screens in iTunes on the computer than it is to do this on the iPad itself, as shown on the left.

Syncing Music

 Select the **Music** pane in iTunes

 Click the **Music** button if you want to sync music from the computer to your iPad

 Leave this button unchecked if you don't want to sync music to your iPad

The available storage on your iPad is limited so the chances are you will not be able to sync all your music across to the iPad.

You could choose only to sync specific **Artists**, **Genres**, or **Albums** by checking the appropriate radio buttons.

Leave enough memory on the iPad for apps and other files. Don't fill the entire memory capacity with music!

 Click on the **Apply** button to start syncing the selected music between the iPad and the computer

If All Your Music Won't Fit

Most of us have more music than will fit on the iPad (you need to leave *some* storage space for apps, docs and other items) and Apple has devised clever ways of allowing us to sync only selected content.

- If your music library in iTunes is small you can probably choose to sync **Entire Music Library**

- You can choose whether to copy music videos and voice memos by checking their radio buttons

- You can also allow your computer to fill all the available space on the iPad with songs, but that will leave no free room for more apps and other files. It's probably best not to choose this option

Make life easier using playlists

 Make yourself a playlist in iTunes (call it *iPad*)

 Drag the tracks you want on the iPad onto this playlist folder

 Under the **Music pane** in iTunes check the radio button for the playlist called iPad

 When you sync, that playlist will be copied to the iPad

Syncing your music is much easier if you create Playlists and Hot Playlists.

DEVICES
- ▶ 🔲 Drew Provan's iPad
- ▶ 📺 Apple TV 28.8.10

GENIUS

PLAYLISTS
- 🎚 iTunes DJ
- ⚙ 60's Music
- ⚙ Classical Music
- ⚙ Ipod touch -> PHONE
- ⚙ Music Videos
- ⚙ My Top Rated
- ⚙ Top 25 Most Played
- ♩ Adam
- ♩ adam williams
- ♩ Apple Jazz Essentials
- ♩ Arabic
- ♩ Birthday new
- ♩ Classical
- ♩ Dancey stuff
- ♩ Drew Provan's Playlist
- ♩ Drew's current favorites
- ♩ DrewVal
- ♩ From Neil B
- ♩ Guitar Signature Licks Of Jimi Hendri...
- ♩ iiO
- ♩ Jazz lounge
- ♩ Jazziz
- ♩ LimeWire
- ♩ Misc backing tracks
- ♩ New Philosomatkia
- ♩ New Session stuff??
- ♩ New stuff
- ♩ On-The-Go 2
- ♩ Ones I forget

Sync Videos

You will no doubt want to watch videos on your iPad. You can buy these from iTunes directly on the iPad, or on computer or Apple TV. You can also sync your own DVDs onto the iPad.

1 Connect the iPad to the computer and open iTunes

2 Click the **Movies** pane in iTunes

3 You can sync the **10 Most Recent Movies** to the iPad, or you can sync **Selected** movies

4 View your available movies in iTunes and click radio buttons for all those you wish to transfer to the iPad

5 Click **Apply** and then **Sync**

6 To remove the selected movies from the iPad you need to *uncheck* their radio boxes in iTunes and click **Apply** and then **Sync**. The movie you have deselected will then be removed from the iPad

Beware

Video files are fairly large so try not to have too many videos on your iPad at one time.

Sync TV Shows

You can buy TV shows using iTunes on your iPad, computer or Apple TV. If you purchase TV shows on your computer you can choose to sync those to the iPad. If you buy TV shows on the iPad they will sync to your computer.

1 Connect the iPad to the computer

2 In iTunes select **TV Shows**

3 Click **Sync TV Shows** if you want to copy these to your iPad

You can copy only **Unwatched** TV shows, or **Newest**, **Newest Unwatched, 3 Newest,** and various other options.

By checking individual radio buttons for TV shows you can choose precisely which content gets synced to the iPad.

Sync Podcasts

You can subscribe to podcasts using your computer (using iTunes Store) or the iPad.

To sync podcasts to the iPad

 Connect the iPad to the computer

 Open the iTunes **Podcasts** pane

 Select to sync all podcasts automatically or choose specific podcasts

4 To remove podcasts from the iPad, uncheck their buttons in iTunes and sync – the selected podcasts will be removed from the iPad

 Click on the **Apply** button to sync the selected podcasts

Sync Books

You can buy books from the iBooks Store on the iPad (many are free!) or using your computer.

Sync books to the iPad

1 Connect the iPad to the computer

2 Open the **Books** pane in iTunes

3 Select to sync **All Books** or **Selected Books**

4 Check the radio button for those you want to sync to the iPad

5 To remove, uncheck their radio buttons in the iTunes **Books** pane and those deselected will be removed during the next sync

Syncing Your Photos

You may want to copy photos from your computer to the iPad. This is very straightforward.

On the Mac, photos can be chosen from iPhoto or Aperture. On the PC you can sync your photos from Adobe Photoshop Album or Adobe Photoshop Elements. Alternatively, you can sync photos with any folder on your computer that contains photos.

1 Select the Photos pane in iTunes

2 Choose the application or the folder on your computer containing photos

3 Select **Specific Albums,** or **Events**, or **Faces**

4 Check all those you want to sync and click **Apply**

5 To remove, uncheck their boxes and at the next sync they will be removed

Getting the iPad Online

The iPad is a fun device for listening to music, watching videos and playing games but to experience the full potential you need to get it online.

Getting online

The fastest connection is Wi-Fi. All iPad models include the Wi-Fi receiver which means you can browse available wireless networks, choose one and connect.

1 Select **Settings > Wi-Fi**

2 Slide the Wi-Fi slider to **On** if it is **Off**

3 A list of available wireless networks will appear under **Choose a Network.** Tap the one you want to connect to

4 You will likely be prompted for a username and password since most networks are locked (if the network is *open* you will get straight on)

5 Check the signal strength indicator which will give you an idea of how strong the signal is

Join networks automatically

If this setting is selected your iPad will connect automatically to wireless networks. This is useful if you move from place to place and have previously joined their network – you will not be prompted each time to re-enter your details. But if you don't want the iPad to join networks automatically, switch this off.

Sometimes you don't want the iPad to remember all used networks (hotels, airports, etc.)

1 Go to **Settings > Wi-Fi** and the select the network you want the iPad to forget

2 Click the right arrow

3 Tap **Forget this Network** and it will be deleted from the list

For a more detailed look at connecting with Wi-Fi see pages 67-68 in Chapter Three.

The iPad may join networks that you don't particularly want to join. Tell it to forget certain networks.

The Preinstalled Apps

Calendar

This app keeps you organized. It is similar to Calendar on the Mac and Outlook on the PC. The interface is beautiful and it's very easy to enter your appointment details. Usefully, the app's icon shows the current date before you click it to open the app.

You can sync your events (appointments) from the Mac or PC using the wireless (iCloud) route.

The Calendar app will be explored more fully in Chapter Nine.

The Calendar app icon will show today's date even before you launch it, which is very useful.

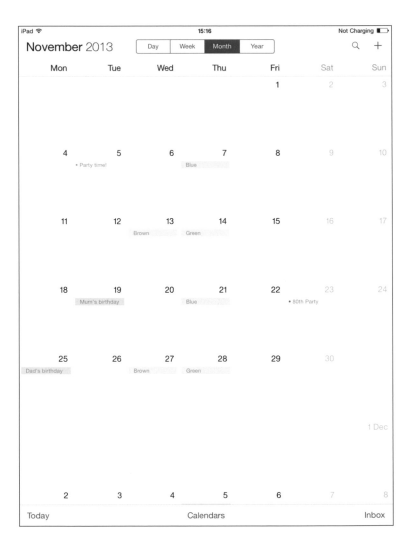

Contacts

This app stores the details of all your contacts. Contacts resembles a physical address book with left- and right-facing pages.

The app works in both portrait and landscape modes.

You can view contacts, add, edit and delete. If you want to add a photo to a contact this is very easy.

There is smooth integration with Address Book on the Mac and Outlook on the PC.

Notification Center

As well as messages popping up on your screen from Facebook, SMS, etc. you can also see all your notifications including anniversaries and other appointments using the Notification screen. From any screen simply swipe your finger down the screen and all your notifications will appear.

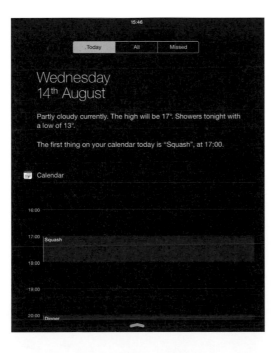

Don't forget

Although the Notification Center itself is not a preinstalled app as such, it takes information from other apps such as the Calendar and Reminders.

53

...cont'd

Mail

Mail is the powerhouse for managing all your email. The Mail app can handle multiple accounts, POP3, IMAP and Exchange. The emails are easy to read and HTML is handled well. The app's views vary depending on whether you hold the iPad in portrait or landscape modes.

Mail closely resembles Mail on the Mac.

Hot tip

Some people say they prefer non-HTML email, but HTML email looks much nicer than plain email.

iPad 🛜		15:04					🔆 Not Charging 🔋
Mailboxes	Edit	1 of 2	🏳	🗂	🗑	↩	✎

Hide

✉ Inbox	3 >	it's a Friday!!!
★ VIP	ⓘ >	
MAILBOXES		? A Friday near the end of Sept looks to be
📄 Drafts	1 >	u. John meadows looking for staff in Nigeria
⚓ Sent	>	me.
☒ Junk	15 >	
🗑 Trash	>	com>
🗄 Archive	>	@yahoo.co.uk>
📁 Apple	>	
📁 Business	>	ere, it's a Friday!!!
📁 Family	>	
📁 Finance	>	ut there always seems to be another book to be written!
📁 Financial	>	moment and I am in charge of the girls as their mother has
📁 IES	>	n't ask!). So I am having to restrict my social outings and I aving my next Edinburgh outing for Kendo's leaving do. from the rather tiresome GKP of course!) - a year out of
📁 Nick	>	the cards? Let me know how the meeting goes - my top tip
📁 Sent	>	opefully I can make the next meeting.
📁 Tax, receipts etc	>	
📁 Trash	162 >	enzie <marcusmackenzie@yahoo.co.uk> wrote:
📁 Travel	>	en chosen....
Updated Just Now		

Notes

This is very similar to Notes on the iPhone and Mac OS X. You can scroll through a list of notes, add new notes, edit, and share using email. You can also sync your notes from the iPad with the Mac and PC using the online iCloud service, if you have an account.

If you find Notes too limiting you can always view the huge variety of third-party apps on the App Store, or you could try a web-based notes service such as Remember The Milk (**rememberthemilk.com**) or Google Tasks.

Newsstand

If you subscribe to newspapers or magazines this new app is where they will end up. Tap the app and browse through your subscriptions.

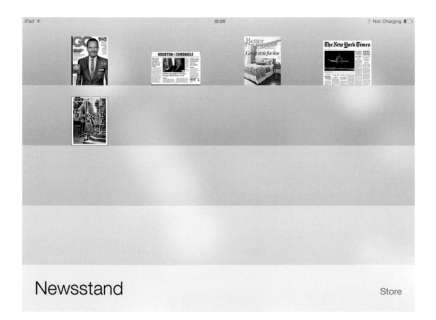

...cont'd

Videos

The iPad is a gorgeous multimedia device. Its large, high-resolution screen makes videos a joy to watch using the Videos app.

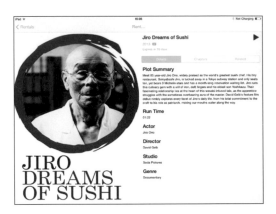

You can watch music videos, movies rented or bought from iTunes or you can copy your own movies across. Plug in a decent pair of headphones and immerse yourself!

Getting your own movies onto the iPad is very easy (this is covered later in the book).

Messages

iMessages from your iPhone and Mac can now be synced with the iPad. All of your devices should show the same messages (much like Skype does).

iMessage on iPhone (above) shows on iPad too!

Reminders

The Reminders app on iOS devices is a welcome addition. The interface is simple and easy to use. Reminders is also available as part of OS X Mavericks and can sync both Mac and iOS devices such as iPad.

Game Center

For all gaming fans, this app can be used to download and play games from the App Store and also play against other people in multi-player games and compare your scores and achievements with other players.

Maps

The Maps app can be used for a variety of uses including looking up locations and destinations, finding directions, locating the addresses of contacts and viewing areas in 3D relief.

...cont'd

Settings app

The Settings app is the central hub for controlling all aspects of your iPad. It is the equivalent to System Preferences on your Mac or Control Panels on the PC. We will explore this in greater detail in a later chapter.

Use settings for:

- Activating Airplane mode

- Connecting to Wi-Fi

- Setting notifications for individual apps

- Reviewing cellular data usage

- Adjusting the brightness of the screen, and choosing wallpaper

- Setting up Mail, Calendars and Contacts

- Controlling audio, Music, Safari

- Configuring FaceTime

The **Settings** app allows you to customize the iPad to suit your specific needs.

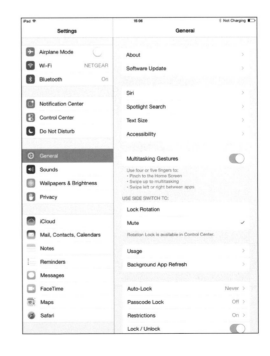

Safari

Although you can download third party browsers from the App Store, Safari is the preinstalled browser on the iPad. It is fast, clean and easy to use. It is very similar to its big brother on the Mac and PC.

You can open several browser windows at the same time and toggle between them.

Bookmarks

You can keep these in sync with Safari on your computer using either iCloud or iTunes.

Safari has an Address Bar/Search box for Google which you can switch to Yahoo! or Bing if you prefer.

Hot tip

If you don't want Google as your search engine – change it to Yahoo! or Bing. Go to **Settings > Safari** and specify your preferred search engine.

...cont'd

Photos

Visually stunning, the Photos app is perfect for showing off your photos. You can review by Photos or Albums and play slideshows. There is also an option to share specific photos.

Music

The Music app on the iPad is very similar to the conventional iPod but because the screen real estate is so large, you can view albums and their covers at a larger size, in all their glory! The layout of the screens is very clear, and you can select your music from playlists, albums, artists and several other ways.

Using playlists and smart playlists you can gain complete control over the content you sync to the iPad.

...cont'd

FaceTime

There was no FaceTime with the original iPad because FaceTime requires a camera, something that was missing from iPad 1. Now, with iPad 2 and the 3rd and 4th gen iPads, (and above) we have the front camera which is perfect for video chatting. The rear camera is also useful for showing your caller what you are looking at.

What do you need?

 iPad with FaceTime and a Wi-Fi or cellular connection

 The other person needs FaceTime on their iPhone, iPad, or Mac. They also need to be on Wi-Fi or cellular network

 Apple ID (i.e. iTunes account, iCloud)

Using FaceTime

 Launch **FaceTime**

 Sign in if not already signed in (you don't need to do this each time)

 Tap **Contacts** and find the person you want to FaceTime chat with

 Tap their **email address** or cell phone number (the latter will start a FaceTime call using their iPhone

⑤ Add to favorites if you plan to call this person regularly

⑥ Tap **Recents** to return a recent FaceTime call

Photo Booth

As the name suggests, this app lets you take photos of yourself as if you were in a photo booth. It also has several built-in effects which distort the image.

 1 Launch **Photo Booth**

 2 Choose the effect you want to use, e.g. Thermal Camera, X-ray etc. If you want a standard image choose Normal

3 Tap the **shutter button** at the bottom and the Photo Booth will take a picture which will be added to your camera roll

Find My Friends

So long as you're not prone to paranoia you can allow your friends to track your location. This way, they can keep track of your movements. I track a couple of friends but don't allow them to see my location.

Don't forget

Although Find My Friends is not a preinstalled app, it can be downloaded for free from the App Store.

63

Restore and Reset the iPad

Your entire iPad contents will be backed up every time you sync with your computer – iTunes takes care of this. For that reason, you should perform regular syncs with your computer, even if you don't want to update the content.

If the iPad misbehaves and you need to restore it you will need a recent backup file to use for the restore.

Restoring the iPad erases the iPad and copies all of your apps, settings, and data from the restore file which iTunes will have created for you (*providing you have synced recently!*).

To restore iPad

 Connect the iPad to the computer

 Make sure iTunes is open and select your iPad when it appears in iTunes under **Devices**

 Select the **Summary** tab

 Select the **Restore** option

 When prompted to back up your settings before restoring, select the **Back Up** option. If you have performed a recent backup you can ignore this

Resetting the iPad
If you have an iPhone you may be familiar with the reset option.

Reset the iPad if it misbehaves.

 Hold down the **Home button + On/Off** button for several seconds

 The screen will go black and the Apple logo will appear on the screen

 Let go of the buttons now

The iPad should boot up. Any problems you had before should have been corrected. If not, try **restoring** the iPad.

3 iPad Settings

The whole look and feel of the iPad is controlled through Settings, one of the apps preinstalled on the iPad. In this section we will look at all settings, from wallpapers to the Music app, getting things set up perfectly for optimal use.

Up in the Air

The iPad is a great multimedia device for listening to music or watching movies on the plane. There are strict rules about wireless and cellular receivers – these must be switched off during the flight. Airplane Mode switches all iPad radios off. Airplane mode is only seen with the Wi-Fi and cellular models.

Turn on Airplane Mode when you fly! This turns all wireless transmitters and receivers off.

Although the new iPad supports 4G, this functionality is not available in every country.

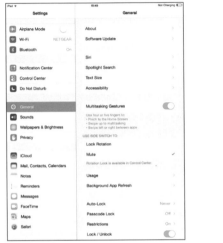

Settings on Wi-Fi model   Settings on Wi-Fi + cellular model

Wi-Fi only models

 Go to **Settings > Wi-Fi**. Turn Wi-Fi **Off** by tapping the **On/Off** button or sliding the slider to the right

 Wi-Fi is now fully off. You cannot receive Wi-Fi signals and the iPad is safe to use on the plane

Wi-Fi and cellular models

 Go to **Settings > Airplane Mode** and push the slider to the right

Wi-Fi and cellular radios are now fully off

For both models, when you are off the plane, go back to settings and slide the slider to the left which switches the radios back on.

Getting Online with Wi-Fi

The iPad is designed to be used online – using either a wireless connection or cellular network. You can use it without Internet access but you won't be able to browse online content, download apps, content, or update your apps.

Connect to a wireless network

 1 Open **Settings > Wi-Fi**

2 Make sure Wi-Fi is set to **On**

3 Choose a network: you will see a list of available networks near you. If locked (most are) you will see a padlock symbol. Some networks may appear "open" and let you connect but when you browse you will be presented with a request for username and password

4 Tap the name of the network you want to connect to

5 Enter the password if you know it

6 You should see a check mark next to the network name showing which wireless network you have joined

7 If your network is hidden but you know its name tap **Other...**

8 You can allow the iPad to join networks quietly without alerting you (**Ask to Join Networks Off**) or you may prefer to be asked before the iPad joins a network (**Ask to Join Networks On**)

No Wi-Fi connection? If you have an iPhone, switch on **Personal Hotspot** (**Settings > Personal Hotspot**). This lets the iPad use the iPhone's cellular connection. Be careful – the data used comes out of your iPhone allowance!

...cont'd

9 You can see the strength of the connection by checking the wireless icon at the top left of the iPad display or in the wireless connection window (in **Settings**)

Setting network connection manually

1 Tap the blue arrow to the right of the network name

2 You can choose an IP Address using **DHCP**, **BootIP**, or **Static Address. Subnet Mask, Router, DNS**, and **Search Domains** are also shown in the window though you won't need to change these

3 If you use a proxy to get onto the Internet, enter the details manually or set to **Auto**. Most people don't use proxies so it is unlikely you'll need to change anything here

Another network setting is for switching Bluetooth on or off for sharing content over short distances with radio connectivity.

Setting Up Notifications

If you have used the iPhone you will be familiar with notifications. These are audio and visual alerts used by some apps. For example, if you use a messaging app you may want to see how many unread messages there are without actually opening the app. Or, if you use an app like Skype, you may want to be shown on screen when someone is calling you even when the iPad screen is locked. By setting up your notifications you can choose how much or how little information you receive in terms of messages, calls, updates, etc.

Set up notifications

1 Open **Settings > Notification Center**

2 Turn **Notifications View** and **Today View** to **On**

3 Under the **Include** heading you will see a list of apps that use Notifications

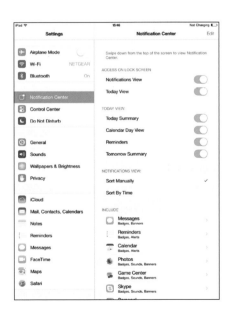

4 To configure Notifications for an app, tap its name in the list

Some apps offer notification by **Sounds, Alerts** and **Badges**. Sounds **On** means the iPad will play a sound when a notification is received. Alerts are messages that display on the screen, and Badges are the red circles that appear at the top right of the app's icon when notifications have been received.

If you want to keep intrusion from notifications to a minimum, switch off Notifications completely or adjust the settings on an app-by-app basis.

Hot tip

Spend some time setting up your **Notifications** to avoid unwanted intrusions by apps sending useless notifications!

Cellular Data

This is only shown in the Wi-Fi and cellular model.

Check cellular data

1 Go to **Settings** > **Cellular**

2 Make sure Cellular Data is **On**

You may want to use **Data Roaming** to get online if you are away from your home country. *Note*: roaming charges for Internet access are high so be careful if you switch this to ON. In general, it is better to leave this switched OFF!

- You can view your account, review your data plan, **Add Data** or **Change Plan** (from pay-as-you-go to monthly), and Edit User Information

- **APN Settings** will vary depending on your carrier

- You can set up a **SIM PIN**

- Under **SIM Applications** you will see lots of services provided by your cellular carrier

Beware

When abroad, keep Data Roaming OFF or your phone bill may be huge – the cost of data download outside your own country is generally very high. Or you may be very wealthy in which case you can switch it on!

Set Up Your Wallpaper

Just like your Mac or PC, you can change the picture displayed at the Lock Screen and the background you see behind the apps. You can alter both of these using the in-built iPad wallpapers or you can use your own pictures.

Apple has already provided some excellent images but you may want more. There are several websites offering wallpapers and one of the best is **interfacelift.com** which offers stunning photos for Mac and PC – these should work on the iPad as well.

Changing the wallpaper

1 Go to **Settings > Wallpaper & Brightness**

2 Tap on one of the **Choose Wallpaper** options

71

There are 34 different Apple backgrounds that can be used for wallpaper. These include **Dynamic** backgrounds that appear to move independently from the apps icon layer above, and **Stills** backgrounds.

3 Select **Apple Wallpaper** or **Photos**, to select a wallpaper from your own photo collection on the iPad

4 Tap to make your choice and decide whether you want the new image as only wallpaper or Lock Screen or both

General Settings

About

This provides full information about your iPad, serial number, number of apps installed, songs, and much more.

Software Update

This can be used to check the version of iOS that you are using and install updates if they are available.

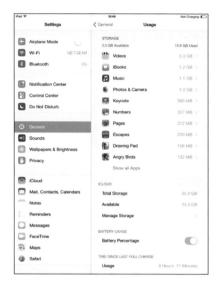

Siri

Use this to set the language and voice style for the Siri voice assistant function.

Spotlight Search

Determines the types of items that appear in the Spotlight Search window.

Text Size

Set the text size for apps that support this function.

Accessibility

Use this to set a variety of accessibility features for vision, hearing, learning and physical and motor conditions.

Multitasking Gestures

This setting allows you to pinch to activate the Home screen, swipe up (four fingers) to reveal the Multitasking bar, or swipe left or right between running apps.

Use Side Switch to:

You can configure the Side Switch to lock rotation, or activate the Mute function.

Usage

This tells you how much data you have sent and received. You can also switch Battery Percentage on here.

Background App Refresh

This can be used to allow apps to be updated automatically when your iPad has online access through Wi-Fi or a cellular service.

Don't forget

There is a specific setting for **Sounds**, where you can configure the alert sounds for new mail arriving, sent mail, calendar and social networking app alerts, lock sounds and keyboard clicks.

Autolock

This locks the screen if there is no input after a set period. You can select between 2-15 minutes or Never. Something around five minutes is probably the most practical. Once the autolock is activated you will need to re-enter your four-digit PIN at the Lock Screen to use the iPad.

Passcode Lock

You don't need to set this but your data will be safer if you switch this to ON. Set a four-digit PIN that you will remember!

Restrictions

Useful if the iPad will be used by children. You can limit access to specific apps and also prohibit the installation of apps.

Lock/Unlock

This can be used to automatically lock or unlock your iPad, through the use of an iPad cover.

Date & Time

Choose the 12- or 24-hour clock. Set Time Zone, Date and Time.

Keyboard

Here you can enable and disable Auto-Correction, Auto-Capitalization of the first letter in sentences, Enable Caps Lock and "." Shortcut (two taps on spacebar generates a period).

International

This allows you to select keyboards in different languages.

iTunes Wi-Fi Sync

This can be used to automatically sync the contents of your iPad with iTunes on your computer, when your iPad is connected to Wi-Fi. In iTunes on your computer you have to also check on **Sync with this iPad over Wi-Fi**.

VPN

Lets you see your VPN (Virtual Private Network) connection if you use one, or the wireless network to which you are connected.

Reset

Use this to reset a setting all of your iPad settings, network settings, the keyboard, the Home screen layout and location and privacy settings.

Hot tip

Passcode Lock prevents people accessing your iPad and its data!

73

Mail, Contacts, Calendars

This is the hub that lets you set up your email accounts, your contacts and your calendars.

Mail

1 Tap **Settings > Mail, Contacts, Calendars**

2 Tap **Add Account...**

3 Decide which type to use if you know this. You can choose from Microsoft Exchange, iCloud, Google Mail, Yahoo! Mail, or AOL. If you are uncertain, tap Other...

4 Tap **Add Mail Account**

5 Enter your full name, email address and password

6 Give the account a **Description**, e.g. "Work Email"

7 Click **Save** and Mail will configure the account for you. Ignore the **LDAP Account** unless you have been told to configure this by your Internet Service Provider (ISP). You can add **CalDAV** and **Subscribed Calendars** if you need to use these

Accounts

You can configure Mail to switch on Mail, Contacts, Calendars and Bookmarks for iCloud (cloud) syncing. You can also switch **Find My iPad** to On if you want to use this feature.

You will see the account information displayed under **Settings > Mail, Contacts, Calendars > Name of email account**.

Review the settings for the Mail app

Preview – how many lines of the email do you want to preview?

Show To/Cc Label – show or hide this option

Ask Before Deleting – switch to **On** as a safety measure, preventing the unwanted deletion of emails

Find My iPad is free so set it up and use it if you lose your iPad.

Load Remote Images – if an email contains images and you want to see these, switch to **On**

Organize By Thread – drag this **On** to view email conversations combined into individual threads

Always Bcc Myself – for blind copies sent to yourself

Increase Quote Level – this indents messages that you forward to people

Signature – assign a signature for the end of each email

Default Account – select a default for creating new emails

Contacts

There are few settings to configure here:

Sort Order – sort your contacts by first or last name

Display Order – same as above

Short Name – select the format for an abbreviated version of your contact name

My Info – view your own details within the **Contacts** app

Calendars

New Invitation Alerts – switch to **On** for these

Time Zone Support – set the time zone here

Sync – set a timescale for syncing your calendar events

Default Alert Times – set alerts times for certain events

Start Week On – set a day for your calendar to start on

Default Calendar – select the default calendar for new events

Safari Settings

Adjusting settings here is like using Preferences or Options on the computer version of the Safari web browser.

Tap **Settings > Safari**

Search Engine – choose from Google, Yahoo! or Bing

Passwords & Autofill – use this to remember your passwords and details entered into forms

Favorites – use this to select items to display as Favorites for when new tabs are opened

Open New Tabs in Background – use this if you want to open new tabs while you are still viewing the current page

Show Favorites Bar – when you want to hide the Favorites bar (this is displayed at the top of the Safari window) switch this to **OFF**

Block Pop-ups – leave **On** to avoid annoying pop-ups

Do Not Track – turn this **On** if you do not want any details of your web browsing to be stored

Block Cookies – many sites insist on allowing cookies but you can clear all the cookies later (see below)

Smart Search Field – this can be used to allow search engine suggestions and preload the top hits when you enter a word or phrase into the Safari Search/Address bar

Fraudulent Website Warning – it is wise to be alerted when you visit potentially fraudulent sites so leave this **On**

Clear History – tap on this to delete details of your web browsing history

Clear Cookies and Cache – tap on this to delete any cookies that have been stored and web page information that has been stored in the cache

Autofill is useful and saves you having to type your personal details on websites.

More Settings

Maps

Distances – whether distances on maps are shown in kilometers or miles

Map Labels – turn on or off labels in English

Preferred Directions – specify whether the default for directions between locations is for driving or walking

Music

Sound Check – this evens out the volume so that tracks will play back at the same volume

EQ – sets the equalizer which enhances the audio output

Volume Limit – prevents hearing damage by limiting the volume of playback, keeping it at a safe level

Show All Music – display all of the available music in the app

iTunes Match – any music on your iPad that is on iTunes is added to iCloud so you can listen to it on any device

Videos

Start Playing – the default is sensibly set to **Where I Left Off** so you can stop watching a movie and resume later

Show All Videos – display all of the available videos within the app

The **Notes** and **Reminders** apps also have their own Settings.

There is a range of **Privacy** settings where you can turn on **Location Services** so that specific apps can use your current geographic location.

...cont'd

FaceTime

Enter the email address you want to use with FaceTime. If you don't want to be contacted using FaceTime you can switch it off

Photos & Camera

Photos – select options for sharing your photos to your own devices with Photo Stream and also other, selected, people

Photos Tab – turn this on or off to show or hide summaries of your photos

Slideshow – use these options to determine how long each slide is played for, to repeat a slideshow and shuffle the photos in a slideshow

Camera – use to turn a grid on or off for the camera, to help with composing photos

High Dynamic Range – use this to blend the best exposures from three photos, while keeping the originals too

iTunes & App Store

This is where you set up your account details for the iTunes Store.

Tap on the account name to see your details, including address, phone number, and credit card.

Automatic Downloads – select which items out of Music, Apps, Books and Updates you want to be downloaded automatically, when you are connected to online services over Wi-Fi

Hot tip

Setting up iTunes alerts is not obvious. To set up alerts go to **Settings > iTunes & App Store** then tap **Apple ID**. Then tap **View Apple ID**. Sign in with your password and scroll down to **My Alerts**. Set up your alerts from the options shown.

Don't forget

There are also settings for social networking sites, including Facebook and Twitter, that enable you to log in to these accounts and link them to iOS 7.

4 Browsing the Web

Browsing the Web is probably the most popular activity on desktop and laptop computers so it comes as no surprise that the same is true of the iPad. Safari is preinstalled on the iPad and is a clean, fast browser that will more than satisfy all of your browsing needs.

Around Safari

The Safari app is the default web browser on the iPad.
This can be used to view web pages, save favorites and read pages with the Reader function. To start using Safari:

 Tap once on the **Safari** app

 Tap on the Search/Address Bar at the top of the Safari window. Type a web page address

| nationalgeographic.com — National Geographic | ⊗ | Cancel |

 Tap on the **Go** button on the keyboard to open the web page

Go

4 Also, suggested options appear as you type. Tap on one of these to go to that page

nationalgeographic.com — National Geographic

Top Hits
National Geographic
nationalgeographic.com
National Geographic - Kids
nationalgeographic.com/kids/
Google Search
🔍 national

5 The selected web page opens in Safari

Navigating Pages

When you are viewing pages within Safari there are a number of functions that can be used:

1 Tap once on these buttons to move forward and back between web pages that have been visited

2 Tap once here to view Bookmarked pages, Reading List pages and Shared Links

3 Tap once here to add a bookmark, add to a reading list, add an icon to your iPad home screen, email a link to a page, tweet a page, send it to Facebook or print a page

4 Tap once here to add a new tab

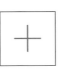

5 Tap once on a link on a page to open it. Tap and hold to access additional options, to open in a new tab, add to a Reading List or copy the link

6 Tap and hold on an image and tap once on **Save Image** or **Copy**

Tap and hold on the **Forward** and **Back** buttons to view lists of previously-visited pages in these directions.

The **Reading List** is similar to bookmarks and you can use it to save pages that you want to read later. Also, you can read them when you are offline. The Reading List can be accessed from the button in Step 2.

Opening New Tabs

Safari supports tabbed browsing, which means that you can open separate pages within the same window and access them by tapping on each tab at the top of the page:

The items that appear in the Favorites window can be determined within **Settings > Safari** and tapping once on the **Favorites** link.

If there are too many items to be displayed on the Favorites Bar, tap once on this button to view the other items.

1 Tap here to open a new tab for another page

2 Open a new page by entering a web address into the Address Bar, or tap on one of the thumbnails in the **Favorites** window

3 Tap on the tab headings to move between tabbed pages

4 Tap once on the cross at the top of a tab to close it

Safari History

All of your browsing will leave a history trail behind. This is useful if you want to revisit sites (*you should have saved a bookmark!*). Over time, the history list will become huge so it's a good idea to clear this from time to time. In addition, other people using your iPad can see your history and there may be sites you visit which you would prefer to keep private!

Clear the history

1 Go to **Settings > Safari**

2 Tap **Clear History**

3 You will be asked to confirm this action

4 Tap **Clear** and the history will be cleared

Add Links to Home Screen

The various iPad screens are home to all of your apps, but you can also add web pages as buttons to the Home screen to make finding and opening these easier. You wouldn't want all of your saved websites to be added to the Home screen or you would have no room for actual apps. But for websites that are very important, or that you visit regularly, consider adding them to the Home screen.

 Navigate to a site you want to save

 Tap the **Share** icon

Choose **Add to Home Screen**

 Name the saved link

The web page will resemble an app on the Home screen

Tap it and it will open Safari and take you straight to the correct web page

Safari Privacy

We have already looked at the History and clearing this from time to time. The other item worth clearing on the iPad (and regular computer browsers, for that matter) is the Cookies file. This is a file containing sites you have visited and the entries are made by the sites themselves. They don't necessarily do any major harm but for reasons of privacy it is a good idea to clear Cookies periodically.

1 Go to **Settings > Safari** – Tap **Clear Cookies and Data**

2 You will be asked to confirm this action

3 Tap **Clear** and the Cookies will be cleared

4 That's it! The Cookie list is now empty

Hot tip

For peace of mind, clear Cookies and Cache from time to time.

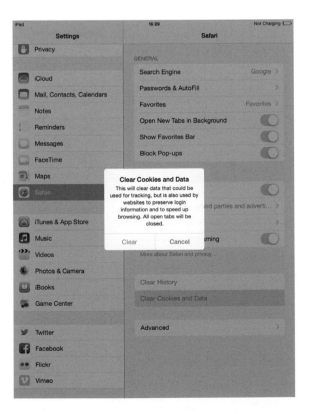

Other Web Browsers

Safari is the default pre-installed browser on the iPad but there are others which include:

- Opera Mini (*shown below*)
- Atomic Web
- Privately
- Mercury Web Browser
- Safe Browser
- Browser plus

Some of these are written specifically for the iPad while others are for the iPhone but can be used on the iPad.

What are the advantages of using third-party browsers?

- Many offer private browsing (no history retained)
- If you get bored with Safari and fancy a change try out one of these other ones and see if it suits your needs better

5 Mail

Love it or loathe it, email is a fact of life. We need to deal with email at work and at home. Mail on the iPad makes reading and sending emails a pleasure and in this chapter we will look at how to set up your accounts, manage your Inbox, and make the most of IMAP email.

What is Mail?

We spend much of our time on PCs and Macs checking and sending emails. This is true also of mobile devices like the iPhone, BlackBerry and other handhelds. So, not surprisingly, a fair amount of your time on the iPad will be spent doing emails.

The Mail app built in to the iPad is a feature-rich program that is easy to set up and use. It is similar to Mail, which comes with every Mac PowerBook and Mac desktop, although a few features are lacking. There's no stationery option on the iPad version and you can't have multiple signatures.

Setting up an Email Account

1 Go to **Settings > Mail, Contacts, Calendars** and tap on the **Add Account** link

2 You will see a list of options

3 Choose the one that matches your email account

4 If you can't see it select **Other** – enter your details including email address and password. The program will work out the rest for you

POP or IMAP?

For most people these are fairly confusing terms but it's worth having a look at both types before setting your accounts up. POP stands for *Post Office Protocol* and IMAP means *Internet Message Access Protocol*. These are the two most common standards for email retrieval. POP3 is the current version of POP and is used for web-based email such as Google Mail. Rather than look at the nuts and bolts of these two systems we can summarize the pros and cons of each.

For Mail, IMAP email offers many advantages over POP3.

IMAP lets you see all of your emails using any machine

If you use multiple computers – including handhelds such as BlackBerry or iPad – IMAP allows you to see your various mail folders from any device. The folder structure and the emails within the folders are the same because the folders and emails are kept on a central server (*not* on your computer or iPad).

iPad 🛜		
Mailboxes		Edit
📭 All Inboxes	3	>
📭 iCloud	3	>
📭 nickvandome@googlemail....		>
★ VIP	ⓘ	>

When you set up a POP3 account you will see folders for Inbox, Sent Mail, Trash but no subfolders or the opportunity to create subfolders to categorize and file your emails. But with an IMAP account you can create as many folders and subfolders (and sub-subfolders) as you like and file all of your emails. You can browse all of your IMAP folders and emails on the iPad and transfer new emails into their respective folders, just as you would with paper mail using a file cabinet. There is a downside to IMAP though – since the emails are stored on a server which may be in the US (iCloud emails are currently stored in California) if you have no Internet connection you may not be able to see your emails.

So, which should you use?

If your email provider, e.g. Apple (iCloud), provides IMAP then select that. If POP3 is the only option you have, there's not much you can do to change this. For those of us wishing to archive emails and retrieve them months or years later IMAP is the best possible solution.

Composing an Email

① Open **Mail** by tapping its icon and decide which account you want to use (if you have more than one) by tapping **Accounts** and choosing the one you want to use

② Tap the **New email** icon

③ Enter the name of the recipient. As you start typing, Mail will present you with a list of possible options. Choose the recipient from the list if it's there

④ Tap the **Subject** box and enter subject here

⑤ Tap the main body of the email and type the text of your email

You can add signatures to your emails (Go to **Settings > Mail, Contacts, Calendars > Signature**). You can choose one generic signature or create a specific signature for each email account.

Type (or use Voice Dictation – see icon to left of keyboard if on Wi-Fi)

Mail will spot mistakes and suggest the correct word

⑥ If you want to copy someone in on the email use the **Cc** box. To send a blind copy (the email recipient cannot see that a blind copy has been sent to another person, hence the term "blind") tap the **Bcc** box

7 Check the **spelling** – any errors will be underlined with a red dotted line. Correct by tapping on the misspelled word and choosing from available options, or delete the word and retype if Mail does not offer the correct word

8 Once you're happy with the content and spelling tap **Send** and your email will be sent

Attach files to an email

At present you cannot attach files in the same way as you would with a regular computer – there's no real "desktop" or filing system you can see in order to find and attach a file. However, it can be done by pressing and holding within an email, see tip.

You can also send files such as documents and photos by email from *within* an app.

For example, in the Photos app there is an option to share photos by email. You can email Safari web pages from within the Safari app, and document management programs like Documents To Go allow you to email files from within the Documents To Go app.

Hot tip

You can add a photo or a video directly into an email by pressing and holding in the body of the email and tapping on the **Insert Photo or Video** button. You can then select the required item from the Photos app.

Here, a photo has been opened in Photos. To email the photo, tap the Share icon (bottom left) and select **Mail** from the drop-down menu options.

This option can be found in many apps on the iPad.

Receiving and Reading Emails

Emails are "pushed" to the iPad from the email server if your iPad is online. You can tell there are unread emails by looking for the badge on the app's icon.

Manually checking for email

You can make Mail check for new email by pulling down on the email list.

Reading emails in portrait mode

If you hold the iPad in portrait mode you will see a separate floating account window listing emails in the Inbox.

1 Tap an email in the list and it will fill the whole screen

2 To see the next or previous email tap the down or up arrows ∧ ∨ or tap Inbox again. Next to the word **Inbox** you may see (3) which means you have three unread emails in the Inbox

3 When reading emails you can: **Move** the email 🗀 **Delete** 🗑, **Reply or Reply All** ↩, **Forward** the email to someone else ↩, **Compose** a new email 🖉 and Flag an email ⚑

Reading emails in landscape mode

1 Tap the email you want to read – it will be displayed in the right pane

2 If you want to navigate to other folders in your account, tap the name of the account (top left) and you will see a folder list

3 Scroll up or down until you find the folder you want then tap it. You will then see the emails contained within that folder

92

4 Navigate back up the hierarchy by tapping the account name at the top

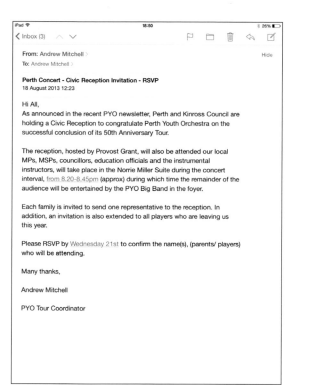

Searching for Emails

Mail provides a simple search box at the top left below the account name. You can search: **From, To, Subject, All.**

Searching for emails across multiple accounts

You can also search for emails using the Spotlight search:

1 Go to **Spotlight** search (press and hold on an empty space on a Home screen and swipe downwards)

2 **Enter your search terms** into the search box

3 Spotlight will then search all of your emails (and will search Calendars, Contacts, Music, etc. unless you have configured Spotlight so it only searches emails)

4 Once the email you are looking for is listed in the search list, tap it and Mail will open and will take you to that email which will open on the screen

Deleting Unwanted Emails

We all receive email spam or emails we don't want to keep.
It's easy to delete emails, either singly or in batches.

Delete a single email

1 If the email you want to delete is open on the
screen, simply tap the **Trash** icon and the email
will be sucked into the trash folder

2 If you are looking at a list of emails in the account
window, tap **Edit** then tap the radio button next to the
email you want to delete. Then hit **Trash**. The brackets
with (1) tell you that one email has been selected for
Delete or Move

3 Another way of deleting emails is to view the list in the
accounts window then drag your finger across the email
from right to left and a **Trash** button will appear. Tap
this and the email will be deleted

Tap on the **More** button
in Step 3 to access more
options, including moving
the email to Junk.

Retrieve Deleted Emails

Have my emails gone forever?

You may accidentally delete an email you wanted to keep. You can get this back!

 Tap the **Name** of the account

 Tap **Trash**. Look down the list for emails you want to recover from the Trash

 Tap **Edit**

 Tap the **radio button** of the email you want to recover

 Tap **Move**

 Choose **Inbox**

7 The message will move from Trash → Inbox

Panic over!

Deleted emails can usually be salvaged from the Trash if you want to recover them.

Get Organized!

Filing emails

 With the email open tap the **Move icon** 🗀

2 Decide which account you want to use to store the email (in this example **Business**)

🗀	Apple
🗀	Business
🗀	Family

3 Tap on the folder name and the email will move across into its new location

iPad	16:31	⚡ 45%
‹ Accounts **iCloud** Cancel	Tap on a mailbox to move this message.	

✉ Inbox 3
📄 Drafts
✈ Sent
🗑 Junk 58
🗑 Trash
🗂 Archive
🗀 Apple
🗀 Business
🗀 Family
🗀 Finance
🗀 Financial
🗀 IES
🗀 Nick
🗀 Sent
🗀 Tax, receipts etc
🗀 Trash
🗀 trashFolder:Deleted Messages
🗀 Travel

Hide

NI

There may be queries relating to your submission, unt via the following link
aspx?uid= and click on the 'All Book
ave any difficulty opening the link, please copy r address bar.

Updated at 16:25

4 Move back to the main account level and tap on the folder name to view its contents

Adding Mailboxes

Different categories of email messages can be managed via Mailboxes. For instance, you may want to keep your social emails separately from ones that apply to financial activities.

1 From your Inbox, tap on the **iCloud** button

2 The current mailboxes are displayed. Tap on **Edit**

Mailboxes	Edit
✉ Inbox	3 >
★ VIP	ⓘ >
MAILBOXES	
📄 Drafts	>
✈ Sent	>
🗙 Junk	>

Hot tip

Messages can be edited within individual mailboxes. To do this, select a mailbox and tap once on the **Edit** button. The message can then be edited with the **Delete**, **Move** or **Mark** options at the bottom of the window.

3 Tap on **New Mailbox** at the bottom of the Mailboxes panel

New Mailbox

4 Enter a name for the new mailbox. Tap on the **Save** button

Cancel	**Edit Mailbox**	Save
Apple		⊗
MAILBOX LOCATION		
☁ iCloud		>

5 Tap on the **Done** button

Done

6 To delete a mailbox, tap on it, then tap on the **Delete Mailbox** button

Cancel	**Edit Mailbox**	Save
Apple		⊗
MAILBOX LOCATION		
☁ iCloud		>
	Delete Mailbox	

6 Photos

iPhoto on the Mac is a great piece of software for storing and viewing all of your photos. The iPad app Photos *delivers rich-looking photos at high resolution so you can view all of your albums as slideshows or share them with family and friends.*

Getting Photos onto the iPad

Because of its high resolution display and rich colors, the iPad is perfect for viewing photos. The iPad supports pictures in a number of formats including JPEG, TIFF, GIF and PNG. But how do you get your photos onto the iPad in the first place?

Importing from a computer program

 You can import from iPhoto or Aperture on the Mac or from Adobe Photoshop Album 2.0 or later, or Adobe Photoshop Elements 3.0 or later

 Use iTunes to configure which albums you want to sync and also remove from selected albums

Using the Lightning to SD Card Camera Reader

 Plug in the Lightning to SD Card Camera Reader

 Insert the SD card from your camera

 Click **Import Photos**

 You will be asked whether you want to keep or delete the photos on the SD card

 View your photos by tapping the **Photos** app

Using the Lightning to USB Camera Adapter

 Plug the Lightning to USB Camera Adapter into the iPad

 Attach the camera using the camera cable

Make sure the camera is turned **On** and is in transfer mode

Select the photos you want to import

Hot tip

Another way to get photos on the iPad is to use Photo Stream. This copies all of your pictures to iCloud and sends copies to your Mac, PC and iPhone!

Don't forget

When importing photos from a camera you can also choose whether to keep the photos on the camera once they have been imported, or delete them.

Adding Photos from Email

You can email a photo to yourself or add any photos you have received in an email.

 Open the email containing the photo or image

 Make sure you can see the image you want to import then tap and hold your finger on the image until you see a pop-up saying **Message, Mail, Twitter, Facebook, Flickr, Quick Look, Save Image, Assign to Contact, Print, Copy**

 Tap **Save Image** and the image will be sent to your camera roll on the iPad

You can save any photos you receive in an email to your Camera Roll.

Saving photos or images from Safari web pages

 Tap and hold your finger on the image you want to save

 Hold your finger on the image until you see a pop-up saying **Save Image/Copy**

 The image will be sent to your **Camera Roll** on the iPad

Viewing Photos

Once photos have been captured they can be viewed and organized in the Photos app. To do this:

1 Tap on the **Photos** app

2 At the top level, all photos are displayed according to the years in which they were taken

Hot tip

If you have iCloud set up, all of your photos will also be saved under the **My Photo Stream** button in the **Albums** section. This enables all of your photos to be made available on any other devices you have with iCloud, such as an iPhone, an iPod Touch or a Mac computer.

3 Tap within the **Years** window to view photos according to specific, more defined, timescales. This is the **Collections** level

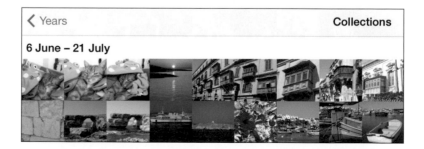

Don't forget

Tap once on the **Photos**, **Shared** and **Albums** buttons at the bottom of the **Years**, **Collections** or **Moments** windows, to view the photos in each of these sections.

4 Tap within the Collections window to drill down further into the photos, within the **Moments** window

Don't forget

For each section, tap on the button in the top left-hand corner to move back up to the previous level.

5 Tap on a photo within the Moments window to view it at full size

Hot tip

Double-tap with one finger on an individual photo to zoom in on it. Double-tap with one finger again to zoom back out. To zoom in to a greater degree, swipe outwards with thumb and forefinger.

6 Swipe with one finger or drag here to move through all of the available photos in a specific Moment

When photos are placed into albums the originals remain in the main **Photos** section. Any changes to the photos in the album will not affect the originals in Photos.

Creating Albums

Within the Photo app it is possible to create different albums in which you can store photos. This can be a good way to organize them according to different categories and headings. To do this:

1 Tap on the **Albums** button

2 Tap on this button

3 Enter a name for the new album

4 Tap on the **Save** button

5 Tap on the photos you want to include in the album

6 Tap on the **Done** button

7 Tap on the **Done** button to finish creating the new album

Selecting Photos

It is easy to take hundreds, or thousands, of digital photos and most of the time you will only want to use a selection of them. Within the Photos app it is possible to select individual photos so that you can share them, delete them or add them to albums.

1 Access the Moments section and tap on the **Select** button

2 Tap on the photos you want to select, or tap on the **Select** button again to select all of the photos

3 Tap on the **Deselect** button if you want to remove the selection

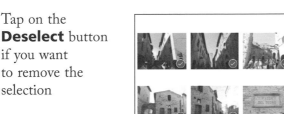

4 Use these buttons to, from left to right, share the selected photos, delete them or add them to an album

Press and hold on a photo to access an option to copy it, rather than selecting it.

To add items to an album, tap once on this button in the **Moments** section.

Tap on photos to select them, then tap once on the **Add To** button and select either an existing album or tap on the **New Album** link to create a new album with the selected photos added to it.

Photos Slideshow

 Tap an **Album** to open it

 Tap the **Slideshow** button (if you can't see the controls, tap the screen)

 Drag the **Play Music** button **On** and tap on the **Music** button to select a song from the music library

 Tap on the **Transition** button to select an effect for when photos move from one to another

 Tap **Start Slideshow**. If you are showing the photos by connecting the iPad to a TV or AV projector use the Dissolve transition

 Stop the slideshow by tapping the screen

Emailing Your Photos

 Open the **Photos** section by tapping on the relevant button at the bottom of the Photos app window

 Open a photo at full size, or tap on **Select** and tap on a photo to select it

 Tap the **Share** icon and choose **Mail**

 Mail will open with the photo already added to the message

 Type email and tap **Send**

...cont'd

Pasting a photo into an email

 1 Press and hold on a photo or image in **Photos**, web page or document

 2 Tap **Copy**

3 Open **Mail** and select **New Message**

 4 Press and hold inside the email body

5 Select **Paste** to paste the image into the email

Emailing multiple photos

1 Open a photo Album

2 Tap **Select**

 3 Select photos to email (up to five at a time)

4 Tap **Share** (top left) and choose **Mail**

5 The photos will be inserted into a blank email

Hot tip

You can paste photos into an email. You can even paste multiple photos into the same email.

Hot tip

iOS 7 makes it incredibly easy to share your pictures with Facebook, Twitter, etc. Tap the **Share** icon and choose the relevant social network. If you have not added an account you'll be prompted to do so.

Beware

You can only Share five pictures at a time using Mail. If you select more than five you will not see the Mail share option.

Adding Photos to Contacts

It's easy and more personal to assign a photograph to your contacts.

 Open **Contacts**

2 Find the contact to which you want to add a photo

3 Tap **Edit** next to the person's name

4 Tap **Choose Photo**

5 You will be presented with a photo album and imported photos

6 Select the one you want to use

7 Move and scale until you're happy with the size and position

8 Tap **Use**

Alternative method

1 **Find a photo** and open it by tapping it

2 Tap the **Share** icon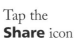

3 Choose **Assign to Contact**

4 Choose the contact you want and voilà – the photo will be placed into the photo box for your contact

Personalize your contacts by adding photographs.

Hot tip

Using the Camera

Because of its mobility and the quality of the Retina screen, the iPad is excellent for taking and displaying photos. Photos can be captured directly using one of the two built-in cameras (one on the front and one on the back) and then viewed, edited and shared using the Photos app. To do this:

The camera on the back of the iPad is an iSight one and is capable of capturing high resolution photos and also high definition videos. The front-facing one is better for video calls.

Photos that are captured with the iPad camera are saved in the **Camera Roll** within the **Albums** section of the **Photos** app, as well as in the main Photos area.

1 Tap on the Camera app

2 Tap on this button to capture a photo

3 Tap on this button to swap between the front or back cameras on the iPad

Camera Settings
Certain camera options can be applied within Settings:

1 Tap on the **Settings** app and select the **Photos & Camera** option

2 Drag the **Photo Sharing** button to On to enable sharing via a photo stream

| Photo Sharing | |

3 Drag the **Grid** button to On to place a grid over the screen, if required. This can be used to help compose photos by placing subjects using the grid

CAMERA

| Grid | |

…cont'd

Taking Photos

Photos taken with the Camera on the iPad can be done in standard format or square format.

 1 Swipe up or down at the side of the camera screen, underneath the shutter button. Tap on the **Photo** button to capture photos as full screen size

 2 Swipe up or down at the side of the camera screen, underneath the shutter button. Tap on the **Square** button to capture photos at this specific ratio

Be careful to keep your fingers away from the camera lens when you are taking photos, particularly when you are using the camera on the other side of the iPad.

111

Use Photos as Wallpaper

Wallpaper, as well as being something you paste onto the walls of your house, is also the term for the backdrop used for the iPad screens. Apple has produced some gorgeous wallpapers for you to use but you can use your own images if you prefer.

 Find the photo you want to use in **Photos**

 Tap to open the picture at full size

 Tap the **Share** icon

4 Tap **Use as Wallpaper**

You will then have the option to use this for the Lock Screen or Wallpaper or both.

You can use your own photos as wallpapers.

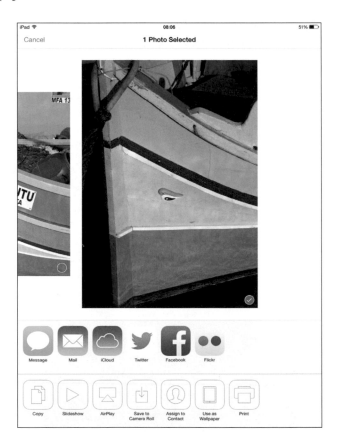

7 Videos

The iPad, with its Retina Display, is ideal for video. The high resolution screen and ease of use make Videos *a perfect app for watching movies you have bought through iTunes or converted from your own DVDs. You can also record video using the iPad's in-built cameras.*

Getting Video onto the iPad

The iPad is a great multimedia device for watching movies, TV shows, video podcasts and other video content. The resolution of the screen makes movies crisp and clear. On the iPhone, video content is accessed from within the iPod app but on the iPad movies have their own app – **Videos**.

There are several ways to get videos onto the iPad

● Buy or rent videos using iTunes on the iPad or computer

● Sync videos from the Mac or PC using iTunes

● Using email if the video is short

● Using iPhoto on the Mac (use the Photos pane in iTunes)

● From a folder on your hard drive

Getting your own DVDs onto the iPad

You may have purchased (physical) DVDs and would like to watch them on your iPad. But how can you get them on the iPad? There are several programs for both PC and Mac that will convert DVDs into a variety of formats including iPhone, Apple TV, iPad, and many other formats. Handbrake (**http://handbrake.fr**) is a free app available for both Mac and Windows platforms that makes the conversion so easy.

Use Handbrake to convert your own DVDs for the iPad.

114

Handbrake has an iPad option at present but I use *AppleTV* which looks great on the iPad and Apple TV.

Playing Videos

To play videos on the iPad you need to open the **Videos** app.

 Tap **Videos** to open the app. Click on the **Store** button

 Tap the **Category** you want to watch, e.g. **Movies**

 Select the one you want

If the video has chapters you can choose a specific chapter to watch.

Where are the controls?

You can use the scrubber bar to move forwards and backwards to a specific place in the video.

 Tap the **iPad screen** while the movie is playing

 The controls (**scrubber bar** and **volume**) will appear on screen

 Slide the **playhead** (filled circle) to where you want to view

...cont'd

The video controls are fairly standard, and are similar throughout iPad apps that play video, including YouTube. The main ones to note in Videos are those that make the screen fill or fit the page. As well as tapping the icons, you can make the video fill the screen by double-tapping the screen while the movie is playing. Double-tapping again will make the video fit (not fill) the screen.

Hot tip

Tap the screen twice when a movie is playing to make it fill the screen. Tap twice again to make it fit the screen.

Pause video	Tap here to pause
Resume playing	Tap here or press center button on Apple headset
Increase/decrease volume	Drag volume slider control or use buttons on Apple headset
Start video over	Tap the playhead all the way to the LEFT or tap here
Skip to next chapter (if video contains chapters)	Tap here or press the center button twice on Apple headset
Skip to previous chapter	Tap here or press the center button three times on Apple headset
Start playback at specific chapter	Tap chapter icon then select the chapter you want to view
Fast forward/Rewind	Touch and hold these buttons
Move to specific point in video	Drag playhead to desired point
Stop watching movie before the end	Tap **Done** or the Home button to quit the Videos app
Scale video to fill or fit screen	Tap here to fill screen
	Tap here to fit the screen

Purchased or Rented Movies

You can rent or buy movies from the iTunes Store. Also, if you have purchased movies using Apple TV these can be synced to your iPad.

 Rent or buy movies from the iTunes Store. Allow the movie to download completely (you cannot watch the movie until it has fully downloaded)

 Tap **Videos** app

 Tap **Movies**

 Tap the movie you want to watch

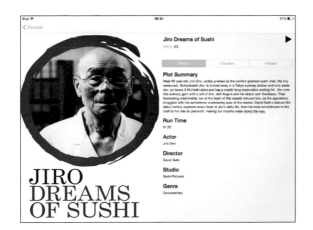

Sync movies purchased on Mac, PC or Apple TV

 Connect iPad to computer

 Go to **iPad > Movies** pane in iTunes and check the movie(s) you want to sync to the iPad

 Click **Apply** then **Sync Now**

Note: The movies you rent *directly* on the iPad cannot be transferred to your computer.

Movies rented on the iPad cannot be transferred to your computer.

Some music CDs have music videos included, or you may buy Music videos on Apple TV or from another source. These should show up in a separate section of Movies (Music Videos).

Removing Videos from iPad

There are several ways of taking movies off your iPad

1 Tap **Videos** on the iPad Home Screen to open the app

2 Tap and hold the movie you want to remove

3 The **Delete** button will appear

4 Tap the **X** icon to delete the movie

Remove a movie using iTunes

1 With the iPad connected to your computer

2 Go to **iTunes > Movies**

3 **Deselect** the movie you want to remove from the iPad

4 Click **Apply** then **Sync**

The selected movie will be removed from the iPad. The movie will *remain* on your computer and if you want to sync it back to the iPad, check its radio button in iTunes.

Hot tip

If you delete a movie on the iPad you will still have a copy on your computer which you can use to resync the movie back to your iPad.

Watch Movies on TV or Screen

You can connect your iPad to a TV or AV projector. You will need to buy an Apple Lightning to VGA Adapter or a Lightning Digital AV Adapter (for HDMI).

Apple iPad dock to VGA Adapter

Hot tip

If you have Apple TV 2 or later you can share your videos using AirPlay wirelessly.

Apple Digital AV Adapter (allows HDMI output and charging of iPad at the same time)

1 **Connect the iPad** to the TV

2 **Select PC** option using your TV's input controls

3 Tap **Videos** to open the app, then select the movie you want to watch

Not all movies can be played
Some movies will not play through the TV – those with DRM (Digital Rights Management) may not play and you may see a warning that you are not authorized to play the movie. The solution (though expensive) may be to buy the movie on physical DVD then run it through Handbrake using the Universal Option, and this should play fine through the TV.

Beware

You cannot play DRM movies on the TV or a screen using the VGA Connector.

Recording and Editing Video

Recording videos using the iPad is as easy as taking still pictures. Once recorded, you can edit your video and trim unwanted footage, email or send your video to iCloud or YouTube, or share your video by sending to Apple TV.

 Tap on the **Camera** app

 Swipe up or down so that the **Video** button is highlighted

 Tap on this button to swap cameras from front to back

Tap on this button to record a video. Tap on it again to stop recording

 Once a video has been captured it is saved within the **Photos** app with the video camera icon and the duration of the video showing on the thumbnail

6 Tap on this button in the middle of the screen to play a video

7 Tap on this button to share a video through the standard iPad options and also social networking sites such as YouTube and Facebook (if you have accounts with these services)

Message	Mail	iCloud	YouTube	Facebook

Slideshow	AirPlay

Hot tip

To share your video on Facebook, go to your Facebook page via the Facebook app or the Facebook site (**www.facebook.com**) and follow instructions to upload videos.

...cont'd

Editing videos

You cannot edit videos with the Photos app but there is a range of apps in the App Store that can be downloaded and used to edit your own videos.

iMovie

This is the iPad version of the Apple video editing app and offers a wide range of editing options and effects.

Finding apps

Access the App Store and enter **video editing** into the Search box to find a wider range of this type of app.

8 Podcasts

Instead of storing podcasts in the Music app, iOS 7 can use an app specially designed like the App Store *and* iBooks Store *where you can browse and subscribe to podcasts. The* Podcasts *app doubles as a podcast audio and video player.*

Podcasts can no longer
be stored and accessed
from the Music app.

The Podcasts App

As with iOS 6 before it, the Podcasts app is separate
from the Music app in iOS 7, where podcasts
were previously stored. The Podcasts app can be
downloaded from the App Store.

Open the Podcasts app

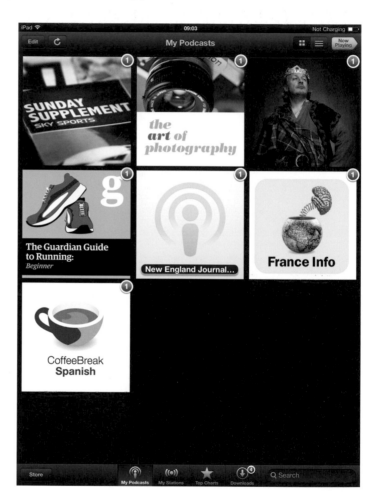

These are the podcasts I subscribe to and have chosen to sync to
the iPad. The number of unplayed episodes is shown in the blue
circles at the top right of the podcast icon. I can change this view
to a list view (*shown on the next page*).

Subscribed podcasts in list view

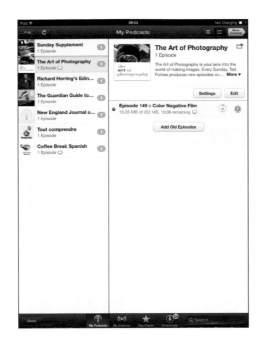

Selective syncing of podcasts

It is very unlikely you will want *all* of your podcasts on your iPad. In the Podcasts pane of iTunes, select the podcasts you wish to sync. When you want to remove, uncheck their buttons and they will be removed during the sync.

Finding Podcasts

You can search for podcasts from within the Podcasts app or use your Mac or PC (via iTunes).

Using the Podcasts app to find new podcasts

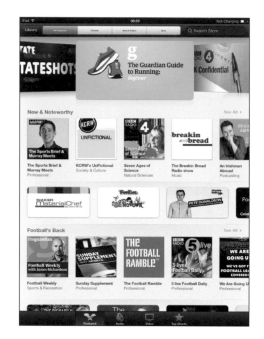

Using iTunes

Use the Podcasts tab in the iTunes window to browse podcasts.

Using Top Charts

A cool feature of the Podcasts app is Top Charts. Almost like using a radio, you can dial up a category and top podcasts in that category are shown.

Here are audio (note audio/video icons at the top) podcasts in the TV & Film category.

Now we are in the Health, Fitness & Nutrition category. Again, this is an audio rather than video podcast.

Listening to Podcasts

If you play an audio podcast you hear only sound, while video podcasts play movie podcasts.

This **Learning Guitar Now** podcast is a video podcast, showing all the usual video controls similar to the Videos app.

This **CoffeeBreak Spanish** podcast is an audio podcast.

9 Calendar

You can never be too organized!

Calendar makes it easy to set up all of

your appointments and sync these to your

desktop calendar program on both PC

or Mac.

Calendar Navigation

The Calendar app has a clear layout and interface, making it easy to enter and edit appointments. The app is designed to resemble a physical calendar, with a left and right page. Each shows different items depending on which view you are using.

In the **Day** view, the left column shows that day's appointments, with the whole day spread out on the right. The **Week** view shows the whole seven days with all appointments clearly labelled. The **Month** view shows the whole month's appointments, and the **List** view shows both right and left pages with the current day on the right and the list of all appointments (the total Calendar appointments) in the left column. The example below is Day view.

Hot tip

You don't need to open the app to see the date – it shows on the app's icon even if it hasn't been opened, just like Calendar on the Mac.

View by Day, Week, Month or Year   Search   Add Event

Tap to go to Today   View available calendars   View invitations

The Calendar Views

You can look at your calendar using **Day**, **Week**, **Month**, or **Year** views.

Week view showing detailed information for each day

Month view

In Month view, you can scroll continuously through the calendar. This means that you do not have to just view a single month on its own, you can view the end of one month and the beginning of the next month in the same calendar window.

Adding Events

You can add events (e.g. *appointments*) to Calendar directly on the iPad or you can use your computer calendar program (Calendar on the Mac or Microsoft Outlook on the PC) and sync the events to your iPad.

To add appointments directly onto the iPad

132

1 Open the **Calendar** app

2 Tap **+** at the top right of the Calendar window or press and hold on a specific date

3 Enter a title for the event in the **Title** field

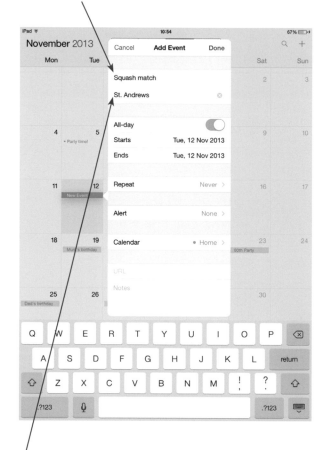

4 Enter a location if necessary in the **Location** field

5 Drag the **All-day** button to **Off**. Tap **Starts** and rotate dials to the required start time

6 Tap **Ends** (One hour is the default since most meetings last an hour) to add the end time for the event. Rotate the dials in the same way as for the Start time

7 Tap **Repeat** if you want to repeat the event, e.g. anniversary, birthday

8 If you want a reminder tap **Alert**

9 Tap **Calendar** to assign the event to a specific calendar if you have more than one

Editing Calendar Events

This is very straightforward. Again, you can edit in your computer calendar program or edit directly on the iPad using any of the views (Day, Week, Month or List). Tapping the appointment once in Day or List view takes you straight into edit mode.

 Tap the **event** to open it

 Tap **Edit**

3 Amend the event, making your changes

4 Tap **Done**

Deleting Events

You can delete appointments using your computer or using the iPad. Either way, it's pretty simple.

 Tap **Calendar** and open the event by tapping it once then tapping **Edit**

 At the bottom of the pop-up you will see **Delete Event**

3 Tap **Delete Event** to delete at the bottom of the Edit window

Syncing Calendar

You can sync all of your events from your main computer to the iPad and vice versa using an iCloud account. In previous versions of iOS this could also be done manually with a Mac computer or PC, but all of the Calendar syncing is not done wirelessly with iCloud.

 Open **iCloud** on your Mac or PC (System Preferences on the Mac or Control Panel on the PC)

 Ensure **Calendars** has a check mark against it

Wireless syncing is by far the easiest and most reliable way to keep calendars in sync.

 On your iPad access **Settings > iCloud** and drag the **Calendars** button to On

 When you add events to Mac, PC or iPad the events will appear on all devices running iCloud

Using Google Calendar

You can add your Google Calendar to the iPad Calendar app. This requires you to set up a new email account using Microsoft Exchange.

The one drawback with this is that you can only have *one* Microsoft Exchange account on your iPad, so if you are already using one for work then you cannot add another.

1 Open **Settings > Mail, Contacts, Calendars**

2 Tap **Add Account...**

3 Choose **Exchange** (not Google Mail!)

4 Enter your email address, leaving **Domain** blank

5 Add a **Description** for the account if you want

6 Tap **Next** (you may see Unable to Verify Certificate – if so, just click **Accept**)

7 In the server box type **m.google.com**

8 Click **Next**

9 You will be asked if you want to Keep or Delete the local (iPad) contents

10 Go back to **Settings > Mail, Contacts, Calendars** and tap the account you have just set up

11 Tap **Mail Days to Sync** and **Mail Folders to Push** (choose the ones you want to push to the iPad)

12 Tap the **email account name**

13 Tap **Done**

Hot tip

You can buy third party apps for syncing Google calendars, e.g. CalenGoo.

Calendar Alarms

How can you be sure you don't miss a crucial appointment? You could look at the Calendar app daily or more often and scan through upcoming events.

But an easier way is to set an alarm, or reminder if the event is really important, for example you might want a reminder two days before an assignment has to be handed in.

On the iPad Calendar, reminders appear as notifications (with sound) on the screen. Set these up by going to **Edit** mode then tap **Alert**. Decide how far ahead you want the alert.

The alert shows as a notification on the screen (locked or unlocked), at the allocated time, and there will be an alarm sound so you cannot ignore the alert.

10 Contacts

Gone are the days when we stored contacts just on a cell phone SIM card. The world of contacts has become much more advanced and Contacts *makes it easy to add and view contacts, making their details instantly available on your iPad.*

Exploring the Contacts App

The Contacts app is a simple but elegant app for managing all of your contact information. The app is designed to resemble a physical address book, showing your **Contacts** and **Groups** down the left hand page with contact details shown on the right facing page.

Groups button   Search box   Add a new contact   Edit contact

iPad 📶   10:12   ⚡ Not Charging ▭

Groups   **All Contacts**   +   Edit

🔍 Search

T
~~Pat Talley~~

Euan **Turner**

V

Robin **V**

Eildih **Vandome**

Lucy **Vandome**

Mark **Vandome**

Mike **Vandome**

Nick **Vandome**

Peter **Vandome**

Robin **Vandome**

Wendy **Vandome**

Vhairi

W

Clare **Wallace**

Isobel **Walton**

Jim **Watson**

David **Watt**

Jim **Westcott**

Claire **White**

John **Willan**

DAVID **WILLIAMS**

A B C D E F G H I J K L M N O P Q R S T U V W X Y Z #

Nick Vandome
"Nick"
Nick Vandome

mobile
07891 123456

FaceTime

home
nickvandome@mac.com

home
1 High Street
Perth
United Kingdom

Game Center
{ Nick729 }

Notes

Send Message

Share Contact

Add to Favorites

Alphabetical thumb tabs   Share contact details

You can also browse Contacts in landscape view but the details are much the same as portrait although the pages are a bit wider.

Tap on a contact in the left-hand panel to view their details in the right-hand panel.

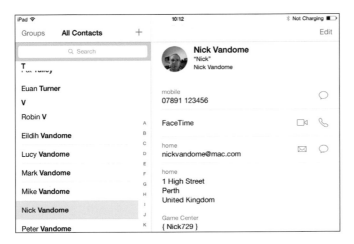

Toggle between Groups and All Contacts

If you have groups, you can access these from within Contacts. Although you can add to a group, you cannot set up a group on Contacts – the group itself needs to be created using your computer contacts app. To view your groups:

141

Beware

You cannot create new groups in the Contacts app, can only add to existing ones.

1 Tap the **Groups** button to view all groups

iPad 🛜	
Groups	**All Contacts**

2 Tap a group name to select it and tap on the **Done** button to view the members in the group

iPad		
	Groups	Done
ICLOUD		
All Contacts		
P3 Squash		✓
Work		

Adding Contacts

You can add contacts directly onto the iPad (these will sync later to your computer).

To add a new contact:

1 Launch **Contacts**

2 Tap the **+** icon at the bottom of the left hand page

3 Enter details into Contact page, adding a photo if necessary

4 Click **Done** when finished

Adding to Groups

With the Contacts app you can also view groups of people for areas such as hobbies, family or work. To do this:

1 Launch **Contacts** and tap the **Groups** button to view all groups

2 Tap a group name to select it

3 Tap **Done** to view the contents of the group

4 Tap the **+** button to create a new entry for the group

5 Enter the details for the new entry (the entry will be added to the group and also All Contacts in the Contacts app)

6 Tap **Done**

7 Tap the **Groups** button and tap on **All Contacts** to view everyone in your contacts. Tap **Done** to view your contacts

Beware

On the iPad, groups in the Contacts app cannot be used to send a group email to the members of the group. However, on a Mac computer the group name can be entered into the **To** box of an email and all of the members will be inserted, using the details from the Contacts app.

Edit and Delete Contacts

Edit a contact

This is easy and can be done on the computer (changes will sync later) or directly on the iPad.

1 Open the **Contacts** app

2 Select the contact and tap on **Edit**

3 Amend the details

4 Tap **Done** when finished

Delete a contact

You can delete contacts by removing them from Calendar, or Microsoft Outlook on your Mac or PC, and when you next sync, that contact will be removed.

Or you can delete straight from the iPad itself.

1 Open the **Contacts** app

2 Select the contact you want to delete

3 Tap **Edit**

4 Scroll to the bottom of the contact page

5 Tap **Delete Contact**

Assigning Photos

You won't want to have photos for all your contacts but for family and friends it is great to have their picture displayed in the contact list.

1 Open **Contacts**

2 Find the contact to which you want to assign a photo

3 Tap **Edit** and tap on **add photo** next to their name

4 Tap **Choose Photo**

5 Select a photo from those stored on your iPad

6 Tap **Use** or **Choose** when you are happy with your choice of photo

Hot tip

Add photos to friends' and family contacts – it makes it more personal.

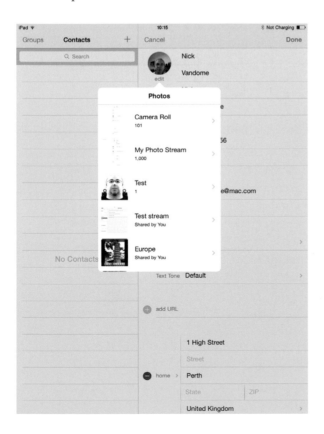

Sharing Contact Details

You can send a contact's details to a friend using email.

 Open the **Contacts** app

 Select the contact you want to share

 Tap **Share Contact** underneath their details and select an option for sharing, such as **Message** or **Mail**

Send Message
Share Contact
Add to Favorites

Send an iMessage to a Contact

Apple introduced iMessage for iPhone and iPad, and now OS X for Mac. Using your iPad you can send an iMessage if you are on Wi-Fi or cellular network. If you use an iPhone you can send iMessages or SMS but the iPad only has the iMessage option.

 Open the **Messages** app

 Tap the **To:** box and enter a contact to message and choose their email/phone number

Type your text and add a photo, if required, (icon to the left of the message box) then tap **Send**

11 Notes

Notes *takes the place of post-its. The app is simple but effective. Not only can you make and store notes on your iPad, you can also sync these to your computer so you need never forget anything again!*

What is the Notes App?

Notes is one of the simplest and most effective of the preinstalled apps. It is much like Notes on the iPhone and Mac OS X. It resembles a blank notepad. What you see depends on whether you hold the iPad in the portrait or landscape position.

In portrait mode (right) you can see all notes in a floating window. The landscape mode (below) is more impressive, with a list of notes in the left-hand panel, with the current note being viewed on the right.

Syncing notes to the computer

The notes you create are intended to sync to your computer. On the Mac the notes sync with the Notes app in OS X and on the PC side the notes sync with Outlook. Notes can be synced wirelessly using iCloud.

Adding a New Note

1   Tap this symbol at the upper right of the screen

2   A new note is generated

3   Type in your text (on the first line, enter something that tells you what the note is about since the first line is used as the title of the note)

4   To finish, tap **Notes** (upper left corner of the window) to take you back to the list of notes

5   Your new note will now be in the list with the date on which it was created, or updated, above it

Sharing Notes

As well as viewing your notes on the iPad, you can email them to yourself and to others. You can also send the note in a Message, as well as copy and print the note.

1 Open the **Notes** app

2 Add a new note or open an existing note

3 Tap the **Share** icon at the top of the screen and select the **Mail** option

4 A new email window will open and the cursor will be flashing in the **To:** field

5 Enter the address of the recipient

6 Tap **Send**

Note sharing options

Syncing Notes

If you have an iCloud account your notes should sync via the cloud to your Mac or PC, and also to your iPhone. Notes on the iPad will sync with Notes on the Mac and Microsoft Outlook 2003 or 2007 on the PC.

iCloud sync

Hot tip

 Open **iCloud** on your Mac or PC (System Preferences on the Mac or Control Panel on the PC)

 Ensure **Notes** has a check mark against it

Your notes can be synced between the iPad and your computer.

3 On your iPad access **Settings > iCloud** and drag the **Notes** button to **On**. Once this has been done, notes created on your iPad should be available on your computer and vice versa

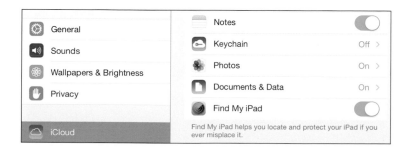

Notes Accounts

Notes can be created to be shared via iCloud, or just created and kept on your iPad.

1 Access the Settings app and tap once on the **iCloud** link

2 Drag the **Notes** button to **On**

	Notes	

3 If Notes is turned **On** in iCloud there will be accounts for **On My iPad** and **iCloud**. The iCloud notes will be shared with other iCloud-enabled devices that you have

iPad 📶

Accounts

All Notes   ›

ON MY IPAD

Notes   ›

ICLOUD

All iCloud   ›

4 If Notes is turned **Off** in iCloud only the **On My iPad** notes will be visible and there will be no other accounts

iPad 📶

🔍 Search

iPad iOS 7   **09:09**

12 Maps

Maps *makes it easy to locate yourself, find places, gauge traffic conditions and get directions to anywhere — on foot, by car and using public transport.*

What is Maps?

If you have an iPhone you will be familiar with Maps since the iPad version is pretty similar although much enhanced. The app shows you a map of where you are, what direction you are facing, street names, directions to a given place from where you are currently (walking, by car and by public transport), and traffic.

The iPad version's large screen shows several views:

- Standard

- Satellite

- Hybrid

- 2D or 3D

To use Maps you will need an active Internet connection – either Wi-Fi or cellular.

You need an active network connection to use Maps to its full capabilities.

The Maps Views

There are four views, each showing slightly different detail. Standard is probably the most useful since it shows the typical A-Z style of map layout.

Don't forget

The different views can be accessed by tapping on the **i** symbol in the bottom right-hand corner of the screen.

Standard view – stylistic but very functional

Satellite view – as the name suggests is a satellite image of the area

Hot tip

Although less glitzy, the Standard view is the most practical in a lot of cases.

Hybrid view – combines the satellite detail with street names overlaid

Satellite 3D view – showing parks, water and other terrain

Finding Places

You can find a location using a number of methods

- Address
- By intersection
- Area
- Landmark
- Bookmark
- Contact
- ZIP/postal code

Maps has the ability to show you places of interest.

To find a location

1 Tap the **Search field** to show the keyboard

2 Enter the address or other search information

3 Tap **Search** on the keyboard

4 A pin will drop onto the map showing location

5 Maps will display places of interest nearby

Zoom in and out

Zoom in	Pinch map with thumb and forefinger and spread apart or double-tap with one finger to zoom in
Zoom out	Pinch map with thumb and forefinger and bring together or tap with two fingers to zoom out
Pan and scroll	Drag the map up, down, left or right

Your Current Location

Find your current location

 Tap on this button

 A compass will show the direction you are facing

 Your **location** is shown as a blue marker

The digital compass

 Compass icon, but compass is white which means it is not active

 Tap the compass icon and it turns blue and now shows North

 Tap again and this icon points to show you the direction you are facing

Tap the compass to find out which direction you are facing. May save you having to do a U-turn!

Want to know more about your current location?

 Tap the **blue button**

 Tap the (**i**) symbol

Details of your location will be displayed

Marking Locations

How to mark locations

You can drop pins onto the map for future reference.

1 Touch and hold any location to drop a pin

2 Touch and hold then **drag the pin** to the desired location

3 To save it, tap the (**i**) icon and then tap **Add to Bookmarks**

4 That pin will serve as a marker for future use

5 To see your dropped pin locations tap **Bookmarks**

6 A list of your dropped pins will appear

7 Tap the one you want to view

Edit your bookmarks

Just like a web browser, you can edit and delete the bookmarked locations.

Clear bookmarks

Tap **Edit** then tap the delete symbol.

Editing and reordering bookmarks

1   Tap **Bookmarks > Edit**

2   You can delete bookmarks

3   Reorder them by holding the right side and moving to new position

Hot tip

Save locations as bookmarks.

Information about a location

Touch the pin and a window will pop up.

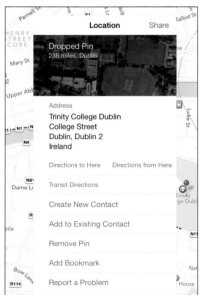

Get Directions

Directions are available for driving, public transport, and walking

1 Tap **Directions**

2 Enter the **Start** and **End** locations into the boxes at the top of the screen

3 If the address is in the **Contacts** list tap and choose the contact

4 Tap this icon if you want to reverse the directions

5 Choose **Directions** for driving, public transport, or walking

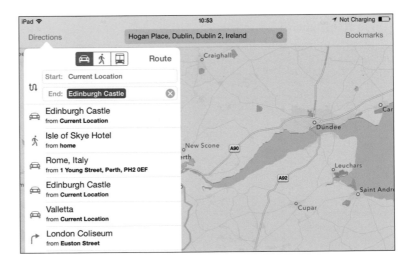

You can view the directions as a stepwise guide or a complete list

Alternative method for finding directions

 1 Tap a **pin** on the map

2 Tap **Directions to Here** or **Directions from Here**

3 **Reverse** by tapping this button

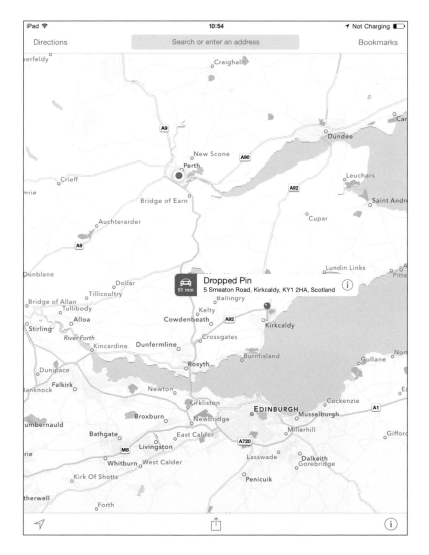

Using Flyover

One of the innovative features in the Maps app is the Flyover function. This enables you to view locations, in 3D relief, as if you were moving over them from above. You can also zoom in and change the perspective. To use Flyover:

 Access a map and select the **Satellite** option

The Flyover function is only available for certain cities around the world, with the majority being in the USA. However, this number is increasing regularly. If Flyover is not available, the button in Step 2 is 3D.

 Tap on this button to activate the Flyover functionality (if available for the area being viewed)

 The perspective changes so you are viewing the map from an angle

4 Zoom and swipe to 'fly over' the map (zoom in by pinching together with thumb and forefinger)

5 Swivel the map by turning in a circular fashion with thumb and forefinger, to view it from a different perspective

Beware

Depending on the speed of your Internet connection, it may take a few seconds to render the map each time you move to the next view with Flyover.

Traffic Conditions

Maps can show you the traffic conditions for locations.
(This feature did not work for all countries or cities at the time of printing.)

 Tap the **i** symbol in the bottom right-hand corner of the screen to view the map options and tap on the **Show Traffic** button

 The traffic conditions are shown as colors:

Green	average speed is >50mph
Yellow	25-50mph
Red	<25mph
Gray	traffic information is not available

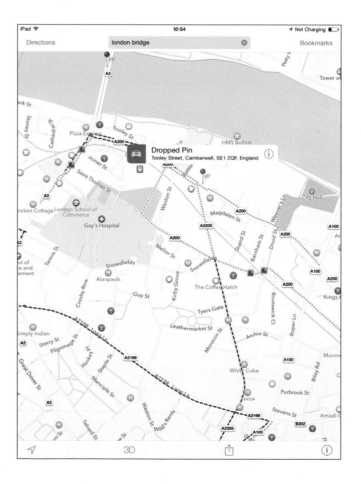

13 Music

The original iPod revolutionized the way we store and listen to music and other audio content. The iPad's Music app is a great music player, and much more.

The Music Interface

This is similar to the standard Music interface on the iPod and iPhone but because the screen is so much larger, the app is clearer and easier to use. You can browse your music by *Artist, Album, Song* and several other ways. Although the iPad has an internal speaker, the music quality is not top quality. You need to attach a decent pair of headphones to hear the full quality of the Music app sound.

Music can also be played with the iTunes Radio service (*only available in the US at the time of prnting*).

iPad 🔋	11:21		✻ 25% 🔋

0:00 ▍   -3:05

◀◀ ▶ ▶▶   The Beatles **Here Comes the Sun** Abbey   Repeat   Shuffle

Store	Songs	Now Playing ❯

Shuffle   ✕

A

	Absent Friends	The Divine Comedy	Absent Friends - Single
	Absolute Beginners	David Bowie	The Singles Collection
	After the Storm	Mumford & Sons	Sigh No More
	Another One Bites the D...	Queen	The Platinum Collectio...
	Another One Bites the D...	Queen & Wyclef Jean	The Platinum Collectio...
	Ashes to Ashes	David Bowie	The Singles Collection
	Atomic	Blondie	Blondie: Greatest Hits
	Awake My Soul	Mumford & Sons	Sigh No More
	Awake My Soul	Mumford & Sons	Sigh No More

B

	Barcelona	Queen & Montserrat Ca...	The Platinum Collectio...
	Battery Kinzie	Fleet Foxes	Helplessness Blues
	Beauty and the Beast	David Bowie	The Singles Collection
	Beauty and the Beast	David Bowie	The Singles Collection

Q A B C D E F G H I J K L M N O P Q R S T U V W X Y Z #

Playlists   Artists   Songs   Albums   Genres   Compilations   Composers

By using the buttons at the bottom of the screen you can browse through your music in a number of ways, including by Artist, Song, Album, Genre or Composer.

Browsing your library by Songs – Playlists are shown in the left panel, and all the songs on your iPad are shown on the right

Browsing the iPad by Albums – you can see the cover art clearly

If you have created playlists you can tap Playlists and select the one you want

The Composer view – probably the least useful of all the views. Looks much like Artist view

Music Controls

The Music controls can be accessed from the library window or when you tap the cover art for the current track.

The controls are very intuitive and are much the same as for the standard iPod. If the controls are not obvious, you may need to tap the screen to bring them up (the same is true of most apps – when video or music content is playing on the iPad, the controls fade).

The main controls used to play music are shown below. What you see varies depending on how you are browsing your music.

Previous, Play/Pause, Next   Scrubber bar   Volume   Repeat

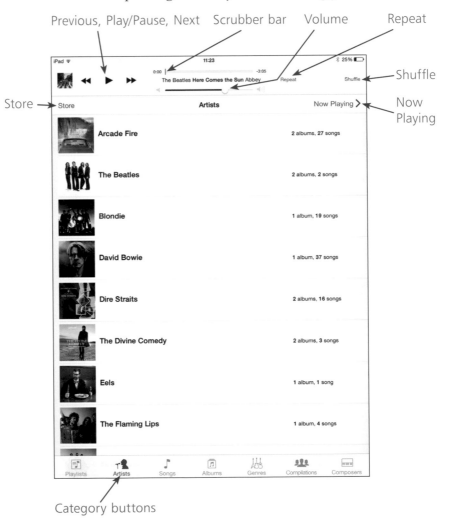

Shuffle

Store

Now Playing

Category buttons

Playing Music

Once music has been bought on iTunes it can be played on your iPad using the Music app. To do this:

 Tap once on the **Music** app

 Use these buttons to find songs by different criteria

 Tap once on a track to select it and start it playing

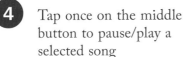 Tap once on the middle button to pause/play a selected song

 Drag this button to increase or decrease the volume

Tap once on this button to **Repeat** a song or album after it has played

Repeat

Tap once on this button to **Shuffle** the order of songs

Shuffle

Hot tip

To create a Playlist of songs, tap once on the **Playlists** button, then tap once on the **New** button. Give it a name and then add songs from your Library.

Hot tip

Music controls, including Play, Fast Forward, Rewind and Volume can also be applied in the **Control Center**, which can be accessed by swiping up from the bottom of the screen.

iTunes Store

This is covered in more detail in Chapter 14.

From the Music app, tap **Store** (top left in the Music window) and you will be taken straight to the store (you will be taken out of the Music app to the iTunes Store, which is a separate app).

Here you can browse available content which includes:

- Music
- Films
- TV programmes
- Audiobooks
- Top Charts
- Genius
- Purchased (items you have purchased previously)

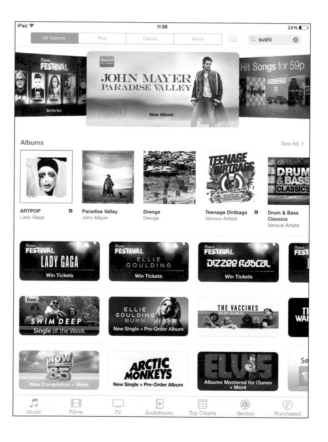

Buying Music

Music on the iPad can be downloaded and played using the iTunes and the Music apps respectively. iTunes links to the iTunes Store, from where music, and other content, can be bought and downloaded to your iPad. To do this:

1 Tap on the **iTunes Store** app

2 Tap on the **Music** button on the iTunes toolbar at the bottom of the window

3 Use these buttons at the top of the window to find music

All Genres	Pop	Dance	Alternative	More

4 Tap on an item to view it. Tap here to buy an album or tap on the button next to a song to buy that individual item

The Suburbs
Arcade Fire ›
Alternative
16 Songs
Released Jul 30, 2010
No Ratings

£7.90

Songs	Reviews	Related

	Name	Time	Popularity	Price
1	The Suburbs	5:15	|||||||||	£0.79
2	Ready to Start	4:15	|||||||||	£0.79
3	Modern Man	4:39	|||||||||	£0.79
4	Rococo	3:56	|||||||||	£0.79
5	Empty Room	2:51	|||||||||	£0.79
6	City With No Children	3:11	|||||||||	£0.79
7	Half Light I	4:13	|||||||||	£0.79
8	Half Light II (No Celebration)	4:27	|||||||||	£0.79

5 Purchased items are included in the Music app's Library

Store	Albums		
S			
The Suburbs	Arcade Fire	16 songs, 64 min
Sultans of Swing - The Very Best of Dir...	Dire Straits	16 songs, 77 min
Sweeter	Gavin DeGraw	1 song, 4 min
T			
Thinking of Me - Single	Olly Murs	1 song, 3 min

You need to have an Apple ID with credit or debit card details added to be able to buy music from the iTunes Store.

Creating Playlists

This is a great way to collect songs you like into one list rather than having to hunt around for them.

 Tap on the **Playlists** button on the bottom toolbar and tap on the **New Playlist** button (towards the top, left of the Music screen)

2 Enter a **Name** for your playlist then tap **Save**

 All of your songs on the iPad will be listed

4 Click (**+**) for each one you want to add

5 When added, the track listing turns gray so you know it has been added to the playlist

6 When you are happy with the selection tap **Done**

7 To edit the playlist, select it and tap **Edit** and remove/add other songs, or change the playing order by moving tracks up and down (touch and hold the track with your finger then move the track)

Hot tip

Creating playlists is the easiest way to group your favorite tracks together.

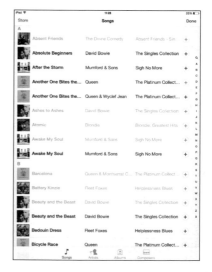

Name the playlist and tap **Save**   Add the tracks you want

14 iTunes Store

The iTunes Store is a huge resource for music, movies, TV shows, podcasts and other media. The iPad version is simple to use so you can browse the iTunes Store and download content quickly and easily.

Welcome to the iTunes Store

This app is a great hub for browsing new music, and renting or buying music and other media including:

- Songs and albums
- Videos
- TV shows
- Audiobooks
- iTunes University classes (directs you to iTunesU app)
- Podcasts

There are more than 20 million music tracks and thousands of movies available for download. Purchases can be made using your iTunes account or redeeming an iTunes gift card.

You will need an iTunes account to buy things from the Store, and for many functions on the iPad. If you haven't got one it would be best to set one up.

First, log in to your iTunes account

1 Tap **Settings**

2 Tap **Store**

3 Tap **Sign In**

4 Enter your **username** and **password**

If you don't have an iTunes account

1 Tap **Settings**

2 Tap **Store**

3 Tap **Create New Account**

4 Follow the instructions to lead you through the setup process

Layout of the iTunes Store

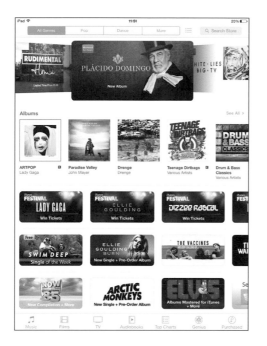

Finding content using Categories

Don't forget

Tap on the **More** button on the top toolbar to view the full range of **Categories**.

Music

Browse music by tapping the **Music** icon at the bottom of the iTunes Store screen.

You can browse:

- All Genres

- Pop

- Dance

- Alternative (when viewed in landscape mode)

- More Categories

Tap on the **Genius** button at the bottom of the screen to view recommendations based on previous purchases.

Genius is a great way of finding new music.

---

iPad 📶   11:52   19% 🔋

Genres | **Music** | Films | TV Programmes | ☰ | 🔍 Search Store

Below find recommendations based on what you've bought from iTunes. In order to get the best possible recommendations tailored to your tastes, turn on Genius from iTunes on your Mac or PC. Genius will introduce you to new music, movies, and TV programmes you'll love.

39 Songs   Songs | Albums   Swipe to Rate Recommendation

Based On Olly Murs **Kiss the Stars** Pixie Lott - Young Foolish Happy (Deluxe E…	£0.99	Based On Mark Salling **Untitled** Jericho - Smoke Signals	£0.79
Based On The Beatles **Jealous Guy** John Lennon - Power to the People - The …	£0.99	Based On Robbie Williams & Gary Barlow **Promise This** Cheryl Cole - Messy Little Raindrops	£0.99
Based On Studio Group **Vem tänder stjärnorna** Eva Dahlgren - En blekt blondins hjärta	£0.79	Based On The Pogues featuring Katie … **Emily** Stephen Fretwell - Emily - Single	£0.99
Based On Mark Nelson **The Water Is Wide** Chris Welch - Songs Without Words	£0.79	Based On U2 **What's the Frequency, Kenn…** R.E.M. - In Time - The Best of R.E.M. 1…	£0.79
Based On The Divine Comedy **To Get Me Thru the Good Times** Echobelly - Gravity Pulls	£0.79	Based On Scissor Sisters **Everyday I Love You Less an…** Kaiser Chiefs - Employment (B-Unique …	£0.99
Based On Snow Patrol **The Sound of Settling** Death Cab for Cutie - Transatlanticism	£0.79	Based On ADELE **Warm Whispers** Missy Higgins - On a Clear Night	£0.99
Based On Emma's Imagination **One Of These Days** Pepper & Piano - One Of These Days - Sin…	£0.79	Based On The Darkness **Little By Little** Oasis - Heathen Chemistry	£0.99
Based On Eels **Seventeen Cups** Kaiser Chiefs - Seventeen Cups - Single	£0.79	Based On Olly Murs **Come On Get Higher** Lilygreen & Maguire - Come On Get Hig…	£0.99
Based On Gavin DeGraw **In Your Hands** Jason Mraz - Love Is a Four Letter Word (…	£0.99	Based On Take That **Heart and I** Robbie Williams - In and Out of Consci…	£0.99
Based On Mark Salling **Wanderful** Jericho - Smoke Signals	£0.79	Based On The Beatles **Instant Karma! (We All Shine…** John Lennon, Yoko Ono & The Plastic …	£0.99
Based On Robbie Williams & Gary Barlow **Fire With Fire** Scissor Sisters - Fire With Fire - EP	£0.99	Based On The Pogues featuring… **Boo Hoo** KT Tunstall - KT Tunstall's Acou…	Album Only
Based On Studio Group		Based On Mark Nelson

🎵 Music | 🎬 Films | 📺 TV | ▶️ Audiobooks | 📋 Top Charts | ◎ Genius | Ⓟ Purchased

Movies

The store makes it easy to browse for movies and to rent or buy these. You can browse by All Genres, Action & Adventure, Classics, Comedy and More Categories.

Previewing movie information

 Tap the **movie** to open an information window which shows the cost of rental or purchase

 Select standard definition (SD) or high definition (HD)

 Tap the **Trailer** image to see a short preview of the film before you buy

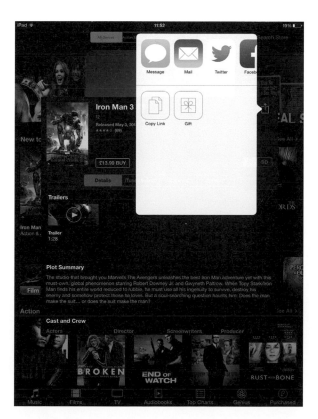 Tap the **Share** icon to send a link to the movie by email or message, or upload to Twitter or Facebook. You can also **Gift** the movie to a friend

High definition versions of movies are usually more expensive to rent or buy that the standard definition versions.

TV Shows

Just like Movies, you can buy or rent TV Shows directly from the iTunes Store.

Browse by:

- All Genres

- Animation

- Comedy

- Drama (when viewed in landscape mode)

- More Categories

Podcasts

There are thousands of podcasts covering a huge range of topics. Many of these are free. You will find all podcasts through the **Podcasts** app by tapping on the **Store** button.

Search podcasts by (at the bottom of the screen):

- Featured
- Audio
- Video
- Top Charts

Other sites to see podcast listings
http://www.podcastdirectory.com

http://www.podcastingnews.com/forum/links.php

http://www.podcastalley.com

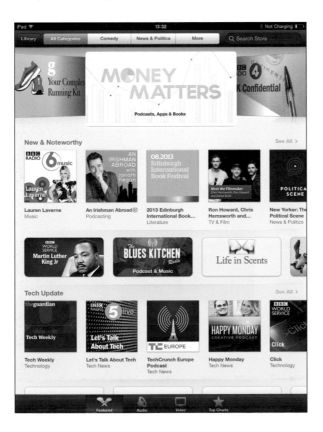

Audiobooks

As the name suggests, audiobooks are books which are listened to rather than read. These are ideal for people who have visual problems.

There are many titles available in the iTunes Store but there are many other sites listing free and paid audiobooks for downloading to your iPad:

- **http://www.audible.co.uk**

- **http://www.audiobooks.org**

- **http://librivox.org**

iTunesU

This is a great educational resource. iTunesU is a distribution system for lectures, language lessons, films, audiobooks, and lots of other educational content.

Finding educational material on iTunesU

Universities & Colleges	Search for content by educational institution (not every university is listed at present)
Beyond Campus	Other agencies offering educational material for download
K-12	Content for Primary and Secondary education. Currently used in the USA, Canada and some Australian territories

iTunesU is now a separate app. You need to go to the App Store and download iTunesU. Once downloaded, you can decide whether to let iTunesU sync content between your devices. You can then browse iTunesU content.

Search for relevant items within iTunesU and tap **Subscribe**.

Genius Suggestions

If you are stuck for ideas for what to buy in terms of music, films, or TV shows you can let Genius make suggestions for you. Genius will look at your previous purchases and make suggestions for you. If you have never bought a TV program using iTunes Store it will say *You do not currently have any recommendations in this category*.

To see the Genius suggestions tap the Genius button at the bottom of the iTunes Store page and select a category at the top.

Above you can see items that Genius has suggested I might buy, based on previous purchases.

15 The App Store

The Apps Store is a vast repository of apps for the iPhone and iPad. The number of third-party apps grows by the day. You can browse and purchase from this burgeoning store right from your iPad and increase the capabilities of your iPad by adding additional functionality.

App Store Layout

You can browse the App Store using the iPad *or* your computer (from within iTunes on the Mac or PC). If you are using a computer, the downloaded apps will be synced to the iPad later when you perform an iPad sync.

Beware

With so many apps available, it is difficult to find new apps easily.

Hot tip

Even if you delete a previously-purchased app from your iPad you can download for free by tapping the **Purchased** tab at the bottom of the App Store screen. Apple will not charge you again for the app.

At the time of printing, over 400 million iOS devices have been sold and there are over 700,000 iOS apps of which at least 250,000 are for iPad! Overall there have been more than 30 billion downloads (all iOS apps).

What are the most popular apps?

These are Books, Games, Entertainment, Education and Utilities.

- Tap **Featured** at the bottom of the screen – if it doesn't show, you may not be on the first App Store screen (tap the back arrow icon to navigate to the first screen)

- Tap **Top Charts** to see the latest apps

- Tap **Near Me** to see suggestions based on your current geographical location

- Tap **Purchased** to see previously-purchased apps

- Tap **Updates** to update your apps

Featured Apps

The **Featured** section displays new and recommended apps. This changes frequently so there will be a lot of new apps appearing here on a regular basis.

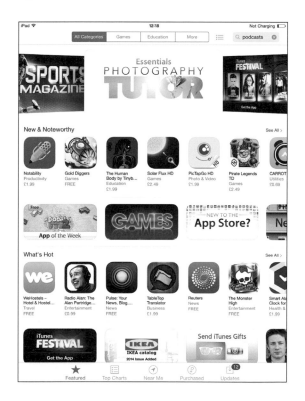

Within the **Featured** section are various categories that can help you further refine your app search:

New & Noteworthy
This shows the apps deemed to be most newsworthy by Apple.

What's Hot
This is a selection of the most popular apps currently being downloaded in the App Store.

Must-Have Collections
Recommended apps, grouped together according to subjects.

Previous Editors' Choice
Previously recommended apps that are still deemed to be worthy of being flagged up to users.

Top Charts

These apps are the most popular. The screen shows the **Top Paid** and **Top Grossing** apps on the left-hand side and the **Free** apps are on the right-hand side.

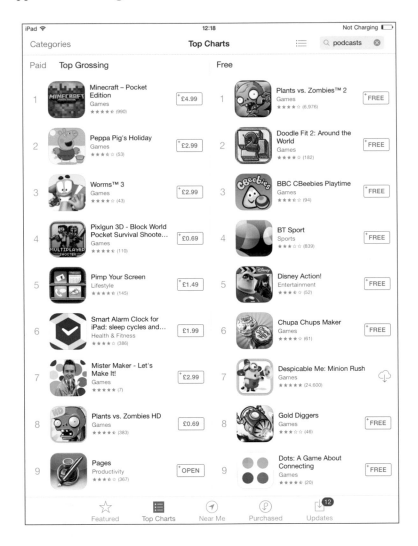

Categories

There are currently 23 categories of apps. This helps (slightly) to find what you're looking for but with more than 700,000 apps, finding an app can be quite difficult! For example, if you tap Lifestyle, you will see more than 2000 apps listed!

As shown on Page 184, it may be easier to browse and find apps using iTunes on your PC or Mac.

Searching Categories

Within **Featured**, the Categories are listed in the top toolbar of the Apps Store. **Games**, **Education** and **Newsstand** have their own buttons and the rest of the categories can be accessed from the **More** button.

Hot tip

There are magazines and books listing and reviewing apps. Consider investing in one of these to help you find useful apps.

Within **Top Charts,** tap on the **Categories** button to view the categories from there.

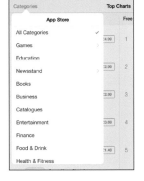

Tap on a category to view the items within it.

Near Me

This is a feature which suggests appropriate apps according to your current geographic location. To use this:

1 Tap on the **Near Me** button on the toolbar at the bottom of the App Store

2 Tap on the **Show Popular Apps Near Me** link

Depending on your location, there may not be any apps featured in the **Near Me** section.

3 Tap on the **OK** button to enable the App Store to use your location (**Location Services** have to be turned On)

4 Recommendations will appear in the **Popular Near Me** window, based on your location

Finding Apps

Standard search methods include

- Knowing what you want! Use the search box.

- Knowing roughly where your app is – browse by category.

- Browsing using iTunes on Mac or PC. Check the App Store pane to find what you want. You can download on the computer and transfer to the iPad later.

Use an iPad magazine such as *The Independent Guide to the iPad*, *iPhone Life* among many others. Try browsing websites listing apps such as **appsafari**, **appcraver**, **appshopper**, **148apps**, *i***pad-application-reviews.com**, **macworld.com/appguide**, **appspace.com**

Buying Apps

When you identify an app that you would like to use, it can be downloaded to your iPad. To do this:

Don't forget

Apps usually download in a few minutes, or less, depending on the speed of your Wi-Fi connection.

 Find the app you want to download and tap once on the button next to the app (this will say Free or will have a price)

 The button changes to show **Install**. Tap on this once

3 Enter your Apple ID details and tap once on the **OK** button

Sign In to iTunes Store

Enter the Apple ID password for "nickvandome@mac.com".

password

Cancel   OK

Beware

Some apps have 'in-app purchases'. This is additional content that has to be paid for when it is downloaded.

4 The app will begin to download on your iPad

Loading...

5 Once the app is downloaded tap once on it to open and use it

Keeping Apps Up-To-Date

App publishers regularly update their software, ironing out bugs and making improvements. The App Store makes it very easy to see if there are any updates for the apps you have downloaded.

How to determine whether updates are available

- You should see a red badge at the top right of the App Store app icon. The number in the circle tells you how many updates you have waiting to be downloaded

- If you don't see a badge there may still be updates available. Open the **App Store** app, tap **Updates** and if there are any these will be listed.
If none is available then you will see **All Apps Are Up To Date**

- You can update one at a time or all at once

- You will be asked for your iTunes password

- Once entered, the app updates will download in the background

Hot tip

Apps can be set to install updates automatically, from within **Settings > iTunes & App Store** and drag the **Updates** button to **On** under **Automatic Downloads**.

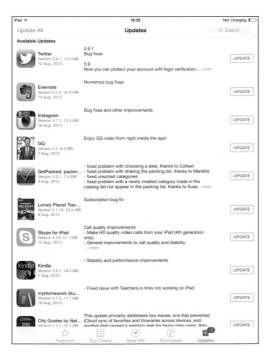

Submitting Reviews

Reviews are useful since they may help you decide whether to buy an app or not.

You can submit reviews for any apps you have downloaded (free or paid).

You *cannot* review any app you do not own.

Beware

You cannot review an app unless you own it.

1 Tap the **App Store** icon to launch the app

2 Find the app you want to review

3 At the top of the screen you should see **Tap a Star to Rate**

4 Tap on the stars to rate the app between one-five stars (you cannot give any app a zero-star rating)

Beware

Even if an app is total rubbish you cannot give it zero stars!

5 Tap in the main **Write a Review** section

6 Enter your text

7 Tap **Send**

8 You can amend the star rating before you hit the Send button

Deleting Apps

There are several ways you can remove apps from the iPad

- Directly using the iPad itself
- Choosing *not* to sync an app using iTunes on your computer

Deleting directly from the iPad

1 Press and hold an app's icon until all the icons start jiggling

2 Tap the **X** on the top left corner of the app

3 A box will pop up warning you that you are about to delete an app and all of its data

4 If you still want to delete the app press **Delete**

5 Press the **Home Button** again to stop the apps jiggling

The app has gone from the iPad but is still on your computer.

You can resync the app back to the iPad later if you decide you would like to reinstall it back onto the iPad.

Delete from within iTunes

1 Connect the iPad to your computer

2 Open **iTunes > Apps**

3 You will see your iPad screen shown in the right panel of the iTunes Apps pane

4 Find the app you want to delete and hover your pointer over it until an **X** appears at the top left of the app's icon

5 Click the **X** to delete the app

Don't forget

If you delete an app in the iPad it will remain on your computer.

Syncing Your Apps

This is very similar to syncing other content to the iPad. You can choose exactly which apps get synced to the iPad by checking their boxes in the Apps pane of iTunes.

1 **Connect** your iPad to your computer

2 Open **iTunes**

3 Click the **Apps** pane. All of your apps are listed in a vertical list alphabetically. If the checkbox has a check in it, the app will be synced to the iPad

4 If you don't want the app to sync, uncheck its box

5 Click **Apply** (in the iTunes window, bottom right)

6 Click **Sync**

Organizing Apps

When you start downloading apps you will probably soon find that you have dozens, if not hundreds, of them. You can move between screens to view all of your apps by swiping left or right with one finger.

As more apps are added it can become hard to find the apps you want, particularly if you have to swipe between several screens. However, it is possible to organize apps into individual folders to make using them more manageable.
To do this:

Hot tip

To move an app between screens, tap and hold on it until it starts to jiggle and a cross appears in the corner. Then drag it to the side of the screen. If there is space on the next screen the app will be moved there.

195

1 Press on an app until it starts to jiggle and a white cross appears at the top-left corner

2 Drag the app over another one

...cont'd

Beware

Only top-level folders can be created, i.e. sub-folders cannot be created. Also, one folder cannot be placed within another.

Hot tip

If you want to rename an apps folder after it has been created, tap and hold on it until it starts to jiggle. Then tap on it once and edit the folder name as in Step 5.

3 A folder is created, containing the two apps

4 The folder is given a default name, usually based on the category of the apps

5 Tap on the folder name and type a new name if required

6 Click the **Home Button** once to finish creating the folder

7 Click the **Home Button** again to return to the Home screen (this is done whenever you want to return to the Home Screen from an apps folder)

8 The folder is added on the Home Screen. Tap on this to access the items within it

16 iBooks

The iPad is competing with some tough cookies in terms of ebook reading. iBooks is an elegant app which lets you browse the iBookstore and save books and PDFs on your bookshelf for reading later. You can read, highlight, use the dictionary, change the appearance of the books and much more.

The iBooks Interface

The iPad is ideal for reading electronic documents including books, and this is a key feature for many people buying the iPad. Just as Apple have made it simple to buy music and other digital content for the iPad, they have done the same with electronic books – ebooks. Browsing and purchasing is simplicity itself. Previewing books before you buy is also possible which saves you buying books you don't want.

The iBooks app provides you with an online **Store** and also a **Library** to store books you have purchased or loaded yourself.

Beware

You won't see iBooks unless you have installed it from the App Store, for free. This is not one of the preinstalled apps.

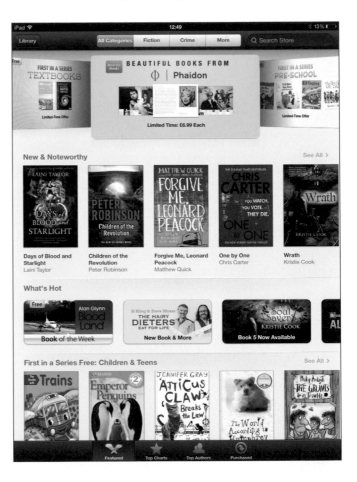

Strangely, the iBooks app is *not* one of the preinstalled apps on the iPad. You need to visit the App Store on the iPad or computer and download the app. iBooks is not available in every country at the time of writing this book.

The library bookshelf

- You can rearrange the books in the Library by tapping **Edit** and then tapping on books to select them

- **Move** a book to your chosen position by holding on it and dragging it to a new position

- **Delete** books by tapping on the **Delete** button and tapping **Delete This Copy** or **Delete From All Devices**

Left: you can browse your collections to see Books, PDFs, etc.

Bottom left: I have tapped **Edit** then tapped one book which I want to delete. I could tap **Delete** and the book would be removed but I've realized I've selected the wrong one!

Below right: after tapping edit I touched one book then dragged it to another shelf.

Open a Book

Books (ebooks and PDFs) are stored on shelves in your Library. Just like a real library, you can browse your collection, open and read books, add placeholders, and more.

 Tap **iBooks**

2 Tap **Library** if iBooks opens on the Store page

3 **Select a book** to read – tap to open

4 Choose a specific point to start reading by sliding your finger along the thumbnails at the bottom. The current page is shown as a slightly larger thumbnail

If you close the app or book, iBooks will remember the place and the next time you open it the book will be opened at the same page as you left it.

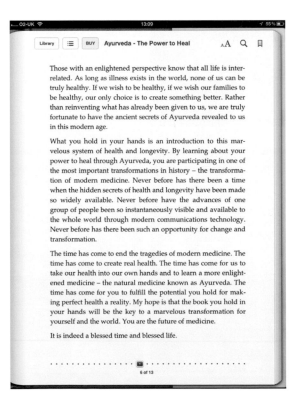

Flicking through a book

 Tap **iBooks** to open it and **Choose a book** to read

 Move through the pages by **tapping right or left margins** (moves you forward and backwards through the book). Or you can **touch and hold the bottom corner** moving your finger towards the top left

 To move to the previous page, touch and hold the left margin and slide your finger L → R across the screen

To move to a specific page in a book

 Tap the **page** in the center. Controls will appear on the screen

 Drag the **navigator** at the bottom of the screen to the page you want

Viewing the Table of Contents

 Tap the page near the center, Controls should appear

 Tap **Contents**

Add a bookmark to a book

This helps you find your place in a book (you can add multiple bookmarks).

While the book is open, touch a word on the page

Tap **Bookmark**

Remove the bookmark later by touching the bookmarked word then tapping **Delete**

Add as many bookmarks as you want to your book – and remove them just as easily!

...cont'd

Want the book read to you?

You will need to activate VoiceOver
(**Settings > Accessibility > VoiceOver**).

Highlighting text

You can use highlighters on a physical book to mark specific pieces of text. The same can be done using an ebook.

1 Open the page of a book

2 Press and hold your finger on a word within the text that you want to highlight

3 Drag the **anchor points** to include the text

4 Choose **highlight** from the pop-up menu. Your selected text will now have a yellow highlight applied

5 To remove the highlights, tap the **text** again and then select **Remove Highlight**

To select an entire paragraph

Tap anywhere in the paragraph with two fingers. The whole paragraph will be selected.

Using the Dictionary

The in-built dictionary is instantly accessible within your books (but not PDF files).

 1 Open the page of a book and tap and hold the **word** you want to look up in the dictionary

 2 Tap **Define**

3 The phonetic pronunciation and definitions will appear in a pop-up box

 4 Tap the page to **close** the dictionary

Hot tip

The Dictionary is not available when reading a PDF.

Ayurveda - The Power to Heal

Those with an enlightened perspective know that all life is inter-related. As long as illness exists in the world, none of us can be truly healthy. If we wish to be healthy, if we wish our families to be healthy, our only choice is to create something better. Rather than reinventing what has already been given to us, we are truly fortunate to have the ancient secrets of Ayurveda revealed to us in this modern age.

What you hold in your h... velous system of health a... power to heal through Ayu... the most important transfo... tion of modern medicine. ... when the hidden secrets of ... so widely available. Neve... group of people been so in... the whole world through ... Never before has there bee... transformation.

The time has come to end t... time has come to create re... take our health into our own hands and to learn a more enlight-ened medicine – the natural medicine known as Ayurveda. The time has come for you to fulfill the potential you hold for mak-ing perfect health a reality. My hope is that the book you hold in your hands will be the key to a marvelous transformation for yourself and the world. You are the future of medicine.

It is indeed a blessed time and blessed life.

A·yur·ve·da | ˌāyərˈvādə, -ˈvēdə |
noun
the traditional Hindu system of medicine, which is based on the idea of balance in bodily systems and uses diet, herbal treatment, and yogic breathing.

DERIVATIVES
A·yur·ve·dic | -ˈvedik | adjective

ORIGIN from Sanskrit **āyus** *'life'* + *veda* *'science.'*

| Search Web | Search Wikipedia |

6 of 13

Find Occurrences of Words

You can search an entire book or document for the occurrence of a specific word.

 Open the page of a book

 Tap and hold the **word** for which you want to find occurrences

 Tap **Search**

 Enter the word you wish to search for

A drop-down list of all pages containing that word will appear.

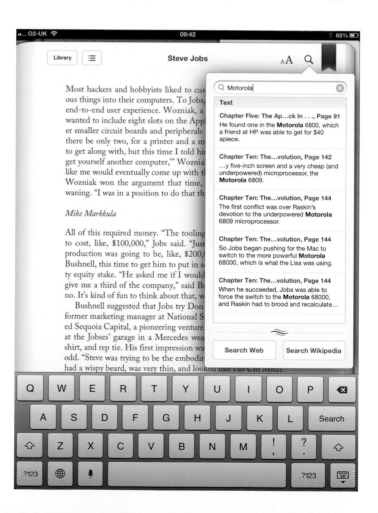

Adjust the Screen Brightness

Depending on the ambient lighting you may need to adjust the screen brightness. For example, if you read in a dark room you could turn the brightness down, whereas outside in sunshine you might need to turn the brightness up.

1 With the page of a book open, tap **settings** (ᴀA)

2 Tap and hold the **slider** to adjust the brightness

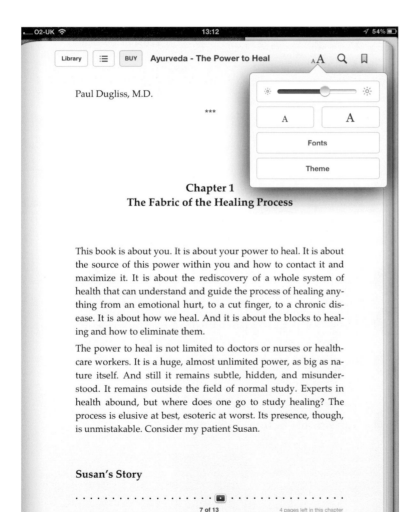

Portrait or Landscape?

The iPad adjusts the orientation of the page depending on how you hold it. If you turn it sideways the pages rotate. This is not particularly convenient when you are lying down.

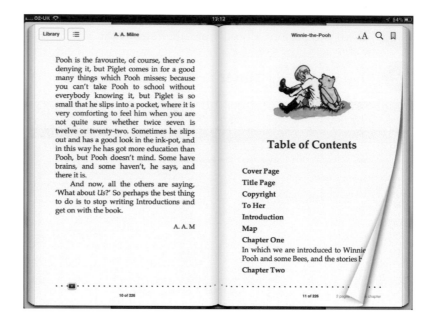

To avoid automatic rotation of the book pages

1 Open a book

2 Hold the iPad in either portrait or landscape mode

3 Swipe up from the bottom of the screen to access the Control Center

4 Tap on this button so it appears locked

Hot tip

Reading a book is one of the times when it is definitely useful to lock the screen, especially if you are lying down!

Using the iBookstore

This is a great resource containing many of the popular titles, with more being added daily. The iBookstore is like iTunes except you buy books rather than music, and there is no rental option. Browsing the iBookstore requires an active Internet connection.

Purchased list

This view shows all the books you have purchased (including those titles which are free).

You need an iTunes account even if you want to download free books.

...cont'd

Browsing is made incredibly easy. You can browse by category or search for specific items.

You can search books by

- **Featured**

- **Top Charts**

- **Top Authors**

- Typing your **search** terms into the search box

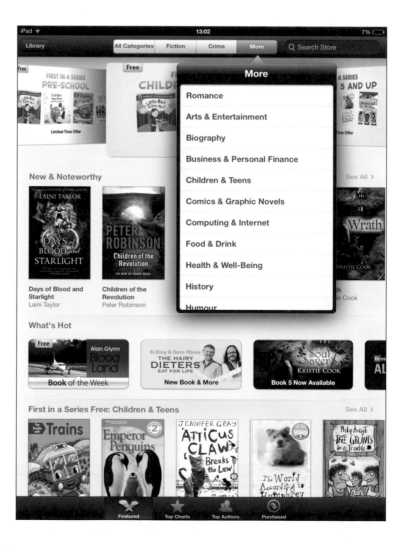

Sample chapters

You can't download music samples in iTunes although you can hear 30-second audio samples before you buy, but you *are* allowed to download short sample chapters of books before you commit to buy. If you like the sample you will probably go back and buy the full title.

Downloading sample chapters

1 Open **iBooks** and find a book that you are interested in

2 Tap the book cover to bring up the information window which floats on top of the current page

3 Tap the **Sample** button and this will be downloaded to your library. This will usually be one or two chapters of the title

Hot tip

Sample chapters are available for most books so you can try before you buy.

209

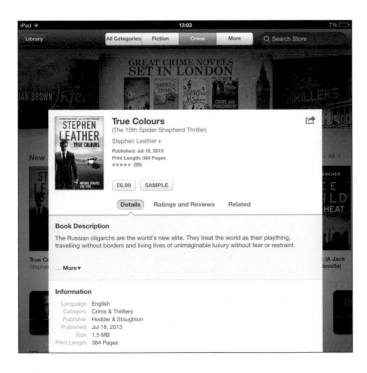

4 Tap the sample in your iBooks Library to open it and start reading

Changing Fonts and Size

Sometimes the font or its size makes it difficult to read a book. With a physical book you cannot change the font but with ebooks you can control the typeface and its size, to make the book as readable as possible.

To change the font or font size

Hot tip

Font too small? Don't like the typeface? Change it!

1 Open a book in iBooks

2 Decide which orientation you will use to read the book – portrait or landscape

3 Tap the **font icon**

4 Tap small or large **A** to make font smaller or larger

5 To change the font itself tap **Fonts**

6 Choose from the drop-down list

7 The book pages may have a light brown tint (**sepia effect**). If you like this, keep Sepia **ON**. If you want clinically white pages turn Sepia **OFF**

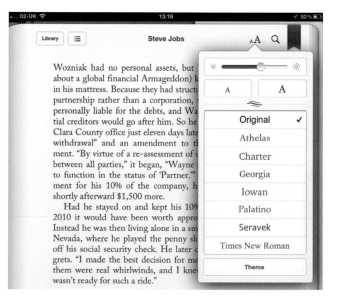

Purchasing Books

Providing you have an iTunes account you can download paid or free books from the iBookstore.

1 Open **iBooks**

2 Tap **Store** if you are currently in Library mode

3 Find a book you want to buy

4 Tap its icon to bring up the floating window showing the price

5 Tap the **gray price box**. This will turn green and will say **Buy Book**

6 Tap **Buy Book** (if the book is free it will say **Get Book** instead)

The Impossible Dead

Ian Rankin ›

Published: Oct 13, 2011
Print Length: 416 Pages
★★★★☆ (104)

BUY BOOK   SAMPLE

Details   Ratings and Reviews   Related

Book Description

Malcolm Fox and his team are back, investigating whether fellow cops covered up for Detective Paul Carter. Carter has been found guilty of misconduct, but what should be a simple job is soon complicated by a brutal murder and a weapon that should not even exist. A trail of revelations leads Fox back to 1985, a year of desperate unrest when letter-bombs and poisonous spores were sent to government offices, and kidnappings and murders we... **More▾**

Information

Language | English
Category | Crime & Thrillers
Publisher | Orion
Published | Oct 13, 2011
Size | 1.2 MB
Print Length | 416 Pages

7 The book will begin to download into your library and the view will change from Store → Library. You will be prompted for your **Apple ID password**

8 Once entered, the book will download

Find More Books by Author

If you have a favorite author or you just want to find more books by the same author you can.

1 Tap the **book cover** to bring up the Information screen with a range of details about the book

2 Tap the **Related** button

3 You will then see any other books on the iBook Store by the same author

Setting up iBooks alerts is not obvious. To set up alerts go to **Settings > iTunes & App Store** then tap **Apple ID**. Then tap **View Apple ID**. Sign in with your password and scroll down to **My Alerts**. Set up your alerts from the options shown.

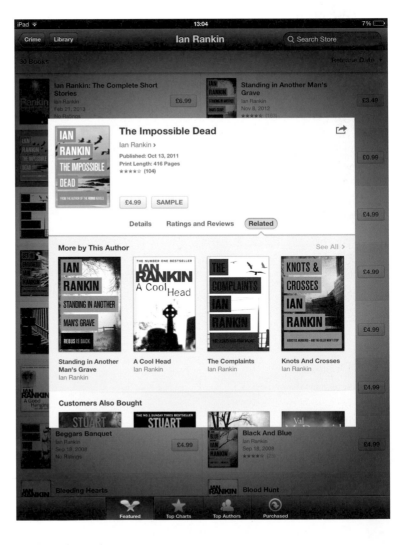

Tell A Friend

You can let other people know about books by sending links to books which they can view on their computer.

 Tap on a book title to view its details

 Tap the **Share** icon

 Select one of the sharing options including messaging, emailing or sharing via a social networking site

If you see something great – share with a friend. It's very easy to do.

4 Depending on the selection in Step 3, information about the item is displayed for the required person, who can then view the item in the iBooks Store, if desired

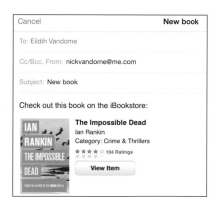

eBooks From Other Sources

You are not completely limited to iBookstore for your electronic books for the iPad.

ePub books

1 Download ePub book (**epubbooks.com**)

2 Add to iTunes (drag and drop the book straight onto iTunes)

3 Connect iPad and sync ePub books to iPad

Other sources for ebooks

- Smashwords (**smashwords.com**)

- Google Books (**books.google.com**)

- Kindle iPad app (**amazon.com**)

- Design your own – many programs allow you to export your files in ePub format, e.g. Adobe InDesign, Storyist, Sigil, and others. Whatever software you use, if it can be saved in the ePub format you can get it onto the iPad. Another option is to save your work as a PDF but you cannot search PDFs for words, or use the dictionary. But it does let you read the document easily

Don't forget

The iBookstore is not the only source of ebooks for the iPad. Most books in epub format will work with the iPad.

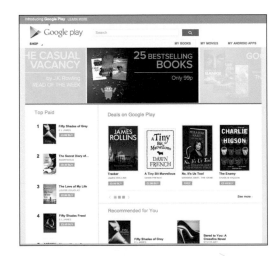

17 The iPad at Work

Sadly, work gets in the way of all this play but the iPad makes giving presentations, writing documents and number-crunching fun! Instead of dragging a heavy laptop to your next meeting, try taking your iPad instead. There's not much you can't do with it!

Storing, Syncing and Editing

The iPad is different to a conventional computer or laptop. There is no "desktop" which means you cannot drag and drop files around and place them in folders, like you would with your laptop.

However, there are still ways of copying files to and from your iPad, allowing you to read and edit text documents, spreadsheets and presentations, and copy them back to your Mac or PC.

There are several apps available that allow you to get files onto the iPad including:

Hot tip

Dropbox is very useful for storing files and is available for PC, Mac, iPad, iPhone and iPod Touch (for more information see page 227). But if you want to edit the files you will need additional software such as Documents To Go or similar. Check out the App Store.

Dropbox (dropbox.com)	Popular on Mac and PC. Provides cloud storage which you can access from any computer. The free account gives you 2GB storage
Documents To Go and Quickoffice	Documents To Go and Quickoffice essentially do the same thing – they let you read and edit Microsoft Office files. They let you keep local (iPad) and remote (on your PC or Mac) files
iCloud	iCloud gives you 5GB free storage. The downside is, it isn't a folder where you can drag and drop your files. Useful for keeping things in sync though
Evernote	Useful for storing clippings, web pages, PDFs, Word files and others. The free account provides 2GB storage and file types are restricted (images, audio, PDF and web pages)

Configure the iPad to view documents

With your iPad connected to your computer, click the **Apps** tab in iTunes. At the bottom of the screen you will see an option for **File Sharing**.

You can configure apps on the iPad to open documents on your iPad. Once you click an app, e.g. Documents To Go, a list of files readable by Documents To Go will appear. Click to select all those you want Documents To Go to open. Then click **Add...**

How you edit your document depends on what app you use on the iPad.

Editing Word documents using Documents To Go

1 Open **Documents To Go** on the iPad

2 Navigate to **Desktop** to add a file from your computer

3 Choose the computer you want to connect to. Tap **My Documents To Go** to see folder contents on the computer

4 Tap the **file** you want to edit (and save locally on the iPad)

5 Once open, tap **Save As**

6 Tap **Location** to navigate back to the local storage, i.e. iPad

7 Tap **Local Files**

8 Tap **Select**

9 Tap **Save**

You can now edit and save the file. In PowerPoint you can add notes and edit your slides (in Outline mode only).

Word files can be read and edited easily on the iPad.

217

Hot tip

Apple's iWork suite is available for the iPad and is very close to the computer version.

Beware

If you use Dropbox to store your word processing documents you will find that although you can open them in Pages you cannot save the changed document back to Dropbox. Annoying? However, for $5 a month you can open a DropDAV account and open and save back to Dropbox. Very easy to set up.

Apple iWork Suite

Apple designed a suite of apps called iWork which includes a word processor (**Pages**), spreadsheet (**Numbers**), and presentation package (**Keynote**).The suite has many functions similar to Microsoft Office. All three apps are available as paid downloads from the App Store.

Pages

1 Tap **Pages** to open

2 Select a **Document** by flicking through the list from L → R

3 Or create a new document with the **+** button

4 Select from the choice of **Templates**

5 **Edit** the text

6 Add **graphics** and then tap media – choose illustrations

7 When finished, tap **Documents** and the document will be saved

8 To **rename** tap the name and enter your own title

9 Tap **Done**

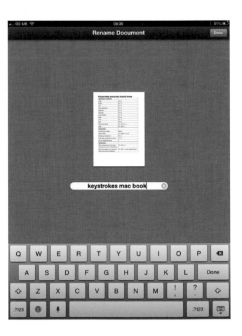

Share documents by tapping the share icon then email, print, copy to iTunes or WebDAV.

Pages will happily open documents created in Microsoft Word and other formats, and can export in several formats including Microsoft Word.

Pages will import Microsoft Word files easily, though some formatting may be lost

Pages shows you a window containing all documents in the Pages "folder". Flick left or right until you find what you want

...cont'd

Keynote

Keynote is Apple's presentation app. It is similar to PowerPoint, although cropping and adding shapes is a bit different. Some aspects of slide design, such as cropping images and creation of shapes, is undoubtedly easier using a mouse but simple slides can be created using the iPad.

Open an existing presentation

1 Tap **Keynote** to open the app

2 Unlike Pages, Keynote only uses landscape mode

3 Flick L → R through existing presentations

4 Find the one you want and tap to open

5 You will see thumbnails down the left side with the slides occupying the rest of the screen

To create a new presentation

1 Tap the **+** button and tap on **Create Presentation**

2 Choose a **Template**

3 Tap **+** to add a new slide – a panel showing available Master slides will appear. Select the one that suits your content

4 Add your text

5 **Save** by tapping **Presentations**

6 **Name** the presentation by tapping its name and entering your own title

7 Save to iTunes or leave on the iPad

Hot tip

Creating new presentations using Keynote on the iPad is cumbersome and I would strongly recommend you create your presentations using a Mac. You can edit these on the iPad later if necessary.

If you save your iWork files (including Keynote) to iCloud you will have ready access from your Mac or iOS device.

Keynote can open PowerPoint files.

Like Pages, Keynote will open Microsoft PowerPoint files. The presentation above was created in PowerPoint and saved before opening in Keynote. Flick right or left to see what presentations are available.

The iPad version of Keynote looks almost identical to the desktop version. Note the thumbnails down the left margin with the current (highlighted) slide showing in the main screen.

...cont'd

Numbers

Numbers is similar to Microsoft Excel. Data is entered in tabular form and can be used to create all types of charts. Numbers can be used in portrait and landscape modes.

1 Tap **Numbers** to open the app

2 **Enter data** into spreadsheet

3 Make sure you have selected the correct data type for your columns (= numeric, = date/time, **T** = text, = calculation)

4 Create **chart**

5 **Save** by tapping **Spreadsheets**

6 **Rename** by tapping its name

7 **Save** to iTunes or elsewhere

Using iPad for Presentations

Just as you would use your laptop to present your PowerPoint or Keynote slides, you can use your iPad once you hook it up to an AV projector or screen.

You will need to buy the Lightning to VGA Adapter. This plugs into the bottom of the iPad and the other end connects to the VGA projector.

Present using an AV projector

1 **Connect** the iPad to the projector using the Lightning to VGA Adapter

2 Open **Keynote**

3 Choose **Presentation**

The file will open in Presentation mode (rather than Edit mode).

The iPad is great for giving presentations and saves you having to drag a heavy laptop around!

If you have access to an HD display you would be better using the HDMI connector (Lightning Digital AV Adapter).

Editing Microsoft Office Files

You have a number of options, such as Documents To Go, Quickoffice, and a number of other apps to edit Microsoft Office files.

1 **Connect** the iPad to your computer

2 In iTunes go to **Apps tab** and scroll down to File Sharing

3 Click the **app** you want to use to edit your Office files

4 Click the **files** on the right to add them to the iPad

5 Open the **app** you want to use on the iPad, e.g. Documents To Go

6 Go to **Local** to see the files on the iPad

7 Locate document and tap to open OR if you want to open in another app, tap the arrow and choose **Open in...** and select the app from the dropdown list

This document has been opened in Pages, but could just as easily have been opened in Documents To Go natively.

Here is the same document opened in GoodReader, Documents To Go and Quickoffice.

In this example, the document has been opened in Documents To Go. The text is perfectly readable, and can be edited, copied and pasted.

Here the document has been opened in GoodReader (a PDF-type app like Adobe Acrobat Reader). The text can be read, copied but not edited.

Here we have used the iPhone version of Quickoffice. The iPhone version runs just fine but the size is not optimized for the iPad screen. In order to try to fill the screen the picture has to be doubled in size, resulting in pixilation of the text.

There is version for iPad called Quickoffice Pro HD.

Get the Latest News

Because the iPad is such a great ebook reader, lots of publishers have made their content available for the Web and iPad. This includes newspapers and journals. Many offer free registration, while others have limited content with a paid subscription for full content.

The iPad is great for reading newspapers, journals, and magazines.

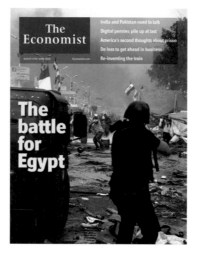

Keep up with politics and economic news

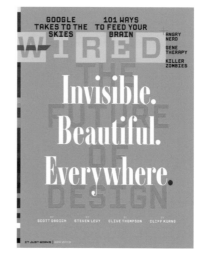

Or tech news with Wired

Medical advances in the British Medical Journal

For the latest in Mac news you can subscribe to Macworld and several other Mac magazines

Organization Apps

In the App Store there is a wide range of organization apps for tasks such as note-taking. Some of these are:

- **Evernote.** As mentioned on page 216, this is one of the most popular note-taking apps. You can create individual notes and also save them into notebook folders. Evernote works across multiple devices so, if it is installed on other computers or mobile devices, you can access your notes wherever you are.

- **Popplet.** This is a note-taking app that enables you to link notes together, so you can form a mindmap-type creation. You can also include photos and draw pictures.

- **Dropbox.** This is an online service for storing and accessing files. You can upload files from your iPad and then access them from other devices with an Internet connection.

- **Bamboo Paper.** This is another note-taking app, but it allows you to do this by handwriting rather than typing. The free version comes with one notebook into which you can put your notes and the paid-for version provides another 20.

- **Errands To-Do List.** A virtual To-Do list that can help keep you organized and up-to-date. You can create your own folders for different items and have alerts remind you of important dates, events and items.

- **Notability.** Another app that utilizes handwriting for creating notes. It also accommodates word processing, and audio recording.

- **Alarmed.** An app for keeping you on time and up-to-date. It has an alarm clock, pop-up reminders and pop-up timers.

- **Grocery List.** Shopping need never be the same again with this virtual shopping list app.

- **World Calendar.** Find out public holiday information for 40 countries around the world.

Printing from iPad

The iPad can now support direct printing (called **AirPrint**).

Apple has provided support for many printers, and a full list can be found at **http://support.apple.com/kb/HT4356**

Available apps that enable iPad printing

- PrintCentral
- PrinterShare
- ePrint
- DocPrinter
- ActivePrint
- Print n Share

Print web page using Print n Share

1. Copy the web page URL to the clipboard

2. Open Print n Share and select **Web pages** from the options at the bottom of the screen

3. Paste URL into box at the top then tap the printer icon

4. Print from screen or from the actual web URL (the latter is probably better)

5. Choose your printer by tapping **Choose**

6. Tap **Print**

18 Accessibility Options

Like the iPhone before it, the iPad has some very effective adjustments which make it easy to use for people with visual and other impairments. This chapter highlights the main accessibility settings which will make the iPad work for you even if you have sight or auditory issues.

Universal Access

Similar to the iPhone, the iPad has a variety of settings that make it easier for people with visual and hearing problems to use.

- Universal Access features

- Playback of Closed Captions

- VoiceOver screen reader

- Full-screen magnification

- White on Black

- Mono audio

Not all features are available for every app. Zoom, White on Black, and Mono Audio work with all apps, but VoiceOver only works with the in-built apps and some apps on the App Store.

Use iTunes to turn Accessibility On and Off

1 Connect your iPad to the computer

2 Within iTunes select **iPad** in the sidebar

3 Click on **Summary** pane

4 Click **Configure Accessibility**

5 Select the **features** you want to use

Hot tip

iPad has many features which make it accessible to those with specific visual or audio needs.

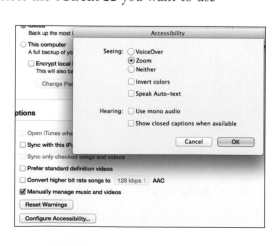

VoiceOver

This setting enables the iPad to tell you what's on the screen even if you cannot see the screen.

 Touch the screen or drag your fingers to hear the screen items described

 If text is selected, VoiceOver will read the text to you

Hot tip

If you cannot see the screen text, VoiceOver will read it to you.

To turn VoiceOver On

 Go to **Settings > General > Accessibility > VoiceOver**

2 Tap **VoiceOver** to turn On or Off

3 Tap **Speak Hints** On or Off

VoiceOver gestures

Tap	Speak item
Flick Right or Left	Select next or previous item
Flick Up or Down	Depends on Rotor Control setting
Two-finger tap	Stop speaking current selection
Two-finger flick Up	Read all from top of screen
Two-finger flick Down	Read all from current position
Three-finger flick Up/Down	Scroll one page at a time
Three-finger flick Right/Left	Next or previous page
Three-finger tap	Speak the scroll status
Four-finger flick Up/Down	Go to first or last element on page
Four-finger flick Right/Left	Next or previous section

Accessibility Features

There are numerous other accessibility features that can be deployed on the iPad. These can all be accessed from **Settings > General > Accessibility**:

Vision

The Vision options include the following:

- **VoiceOver** (see previous page).

- **Zoom**. This can be used to increase and decrease the screen magnification. Double-tap the screen with three fingers to increase the magnification by 200%. Double-tap with three fingers again to reduce the magnification. Drag with three fingers to move around the screen.

- **Invert Colors**. This setting completely inverts the iPad colors, from white on black to black on white.

- **Speak Selection.** This can be used to speak out selected text. Tap on the Speak button that appears.

- **Speak Auto-text**. Turning on this option lets the iPad speak the text corrections as you type.

General	Accessibility	
VISION		
VoiceOver		Off >
Zoom		On >
Invert Colors		◯
Speak Selection		Off >
Speak Auto-text		◯
Automatically speak auto-corrections and auto-capitalizations.		
Larger Type		Off >
Bold Text		◯
Increase Contrast		Off >
Reduce Motion		Off >
On/Off Labels		◯

- **Larger Type**. Use this to allow compatible apps to increase the size of text.

- **Bold Text**. This can be turned on to create bold text on the iPad. It requires a restart to apply it.

- **Increase Contrast**. This aids legibility by increasing the contrast with some backgrounds.

- **Reduce Motion**. This reduces the amount of motion effects that are applied throughout the iPad.

- **On/Off Labels**. This defines the On/Off buttons further by adding labels to them as well as their standard colors.

Hearing

The Hearing options include the following:

- **Subtitles & Captioning**. This determines the style of captions on the iPad, if used.

- **Mono Audio**. Instead of stereo sound, the Mono Audio channels both right and left output into a single mono output. This is useful for people with hearing impairment, since they can hear the output from both channels in one ear. Turn Mono Audio On and Off.

HEARING

Subtitles & Captioning >

Mono Audio

L   R

Adjust the audio volume balance between left and right channels.

Learning

The Learning options are:

- **Guided Access**. The Guided Access option allows for certain functionality within an app to be disabled so that individual tasks can be focused on without any other distractions. For instances, areas of a web page can be disabled so that the page being viewed cannot be moved away from.

...cont'd

Physical & Motor

The Physical & Motor options include the following:

- **Switch Control**. This can be used to set up your iPad for an adaptive accessory such as a mouse, keyboard or joy stick.

- **Assistive Touch**. This contains a range of options that reduce the need for using your hands and fingers as much as for standard use.

PHYSICAL & MOTOR	
Switch Control	Off >
AssistiveTouch	Off >
Home-click Speed	Default >

- **Home-click Speed**. This can be used to adjust the speed for double-clicking and triple-clicking the Home button.

Accessibility Shortcuts

These are settings for selecting options for the functions that are activated by triple-clicking the Home button.

‹ Accessibility	**Accessibility Shortcut**
TRIPLE-CLICK THE HOME BUTTON FOR:	
VoiceOver	
Invert Colors	
Zoom	
Switch Control	
AssistiveTouch	

Index

Q

R

S